THE NEW TEMPLE SHAKESPEARE

Edited by M. R. Ridley, M.A.

TITUS ANDRONICUS

by William Shakespeare

London: J. M. DENT & SONS LTD.
New York: E. P. DUTTON & CO. INC.

Made in Great Britain
by
Morrison & Gibb Ltd., London and Edinburgh

First published in this edition 1934
Last reprinted 1949

Editor's General Note

The Text. The editor has kept before him the aim of presenting to the modern reader the nearest possible approximation to what Shakespeare actually wrote. The text is therefore conservative, and is based on the earliest reliable printed text. But to avoid distraction (*a*) the spelling is modernised, and (*b*) a limited number of universally accepted emendations is admitted without comment. Where a Quarto text exists as well as the First Folio the passages which occur only in the Quarto are enclosed in square brackets [ ] and those which occur only in the Folio in brace brackets { }.

Scene Division. The rapid continuity of the Elizabethan curtainless production is lost by the 'traditional' scene divisions. Where there is an essential difference of place these scene divisions are retained. Where on the other hand the change of place is insignificant the scene division is indicated only by a space on the page. For ease of reference, however, the 'traditional' division is retained at the head of the page and in line numbering.

Notes. Passages on which there are notes are indicated by a † in the margin.

Punctuation adheres more closely than has been usual to the 'Elizabethan' punctuation of the early texts. It is often therefore more indicative of the way in which the lines were to be delivered than of their syntactical construction.

Glossaries are arranged on a somewhat novel principle, not alphabetically, but in the order in which the words or phrases occur. The editor is much indebted to Mr J. N. Bryson for his collaboration in the preparation of the glossaries.

v

Preface

The Text. In 1600 appeared a Quarto with the following title-page :—

" The most lamenta- | ble Romaine Tragedie of *Titus* | *Andronicus.* | As it hath sundry times been playde by the | Right Honourable the Earle of Pembrooke, the | Earle of Darbie, the Earle of Sussex, and the | Lorde Chamberlaine theyr | Seruants. | AT LONDON, | Printed by I. R. for Edward White | and are to bee solde at his shoppe, at the little | North doore of Paules, at the signe of | the Gun. 1600."

In 1611 appeared another Quarto, printed from that of 1600. [It will be observed that neither of these Quartos claims Shakespeare as the author.]

The text of the First Folio is printed from Quarto 2. Apart from the usual emendations and carelessnesses, the only serious difference between this text and the Quartos is that it includes a whole scene (III. ii.) which is not in either Quarto.

Date of Composition. Though the first extant text is of 1600, it is clear that *Titus Andronicus* in some shape or form had for some years previous to that not only been on the stage, but had also been accessible in print. Langbaine, in his *Account of the English Dramatick Poets*, mentions a Quarto of 1594. There is an entry in the Stationers' Registers, under date 6th February 1593, of " A noble Roman Historye of Titus Andronicus"; and an entry in Henslowe's diary referring to a play of that name as being acted for the first time on 23rd January 1593. And a reference in *Bartholomew*

Fair, if we unwisely choose to assume an exactness of chronology in a loose phrase " these five-and-twenty or thirty year," will lead us to put the first appearance of *a* play on the subject several years earlier still. But none of all this gives us the least aid in determining the date at which Shakespeare wrote *Titus Andronicus*, or re-wrote someone else's *Titus Andronicus*, or added a few passages to an existing play, or conducted whatever operation it was that gave us the play now before us. The first allusion which couples Shakespeare's name with the title of the play is that of the invaluable Meres, who, writing in 1598 a comparison of Shakespeare's tragedies with those of Seneca, says " witness for tragedy his *Richard II, Richard III, Henry IV, King John, Titus Andronicus*, and his *Romeo and Juliet.*

Authorship. There has been much dispute, much of it very uncritical, as to the amount of responsibility for this play, total, partial, or negligible, which must be attributed to Shakespeare. Those who cannot endure to think that Shakespeare wrote it pin their faith on a remark by one Ravenscroft, writing some seventy years after Shakespeare's death, " I have been told by some anciently conversant with the stage, that it was not originally his, but brought by a private author to be acted, and he only gave some master touches to one or two of the principal characters." So vague, so late, and so ill-supported a remark, when set against the specific attribution of Meres, and the inclusion of the play in the canon of the Folio, can surely carry weight only to a critic who has made up his mind in advance what his conclusion is to be, evidence or no evidence. " Internal evidence " and " parallels " can, as usual, like statistics, be made to prove anything, as that Shakespeare wrote all the play, that he wrote little or none of it, or that Kyd wrote it. An adequate, though somewhat *ex parte*, statement of the main arguments this way and that will be found in the Introduction to the Arden edition of the play. The writer makes justly short work of those critics whose reason for wishing to remove the play from the canon is that they find it repulsive : but he does not seem to me to meet at all cogently a real difficulty which must occur to any ordinary reader of Shakespeare, the problem "Where in Shakespeare's dramatic career do we feel that we can reasonably put this play?" Put as briefly as possible, the difficulty is this: The play is on the one hand crude and immature ; on the other hand it has a certain strength, amounting sometimes to violence. In the plays which we know to be his the immature Shakespeare exhibits none of this particular kind of strength, and the mature Shakespeare none of this kind of crudity. As against the attribution of Meres and the Folio, I cannot feel that this difficulty can carry the weight which one would wish ; but I think that it needs to be resolved. On the evidence before us I see nothing for it but a regretful admission of the play as Shakespeare's, with such private reservations as individual taste leads us to make.

Sources of the Plot. No single specific source has as yet been discovered. The plot appears to be an interweaving of two related themes which have been shown to have been popular in Europe, one in which there is an isolated figure of a wicked Moor, the other in which the Moor is joined by another figure, and we have a " blackamoor and white lady intrigue."

Duration of Action. There are difficulties about the time scheme, but the ordinarily accepted scheme seems to be as satisfactory as any. It will be noticed that the " additional " scene which occurs in F only demands a whole day to itself.

Criticism. The play has been comparatively little commented on, and most readers will find this silence natural enough. What is the impression which the play makes upon the casual reader? Surely one of crudity and unreality. Aaron is human in his lust, but quite inhuman in his purposeless cruelty ; Titus has a fine vein of rhetoric, but he is drawn in only two dimensions, and his madness barely escapes being ridiculous ; Saturnine is the most conventional of conventional ranting tyrants ; Lavinia is merely a victim to stir horror, not a character who can excite sympathy ; Tamora is more interesting, since her cruelty has a real motive, and her plotting has a certain excitement about it ; the most human character in the play is Titus's grandson. The whole machinery is almost incredibly naive, and the horrors that are designed to make our blood run cold are so crude that they are more calculated to make us smile.

Against this natural impression should be in fairness set a more favourable estimate. Let us go straight to the extreme, much of which seems to me the mere extravagance of criticism, in the Introduction to the Arden edition, by Mr H. Bellyse Baildon. "Up to the scene when she tries to personate Revenge, Tamora's character is magnificently handled. Lustful and ferocious as she is, she has a quality of greatness, such as perhaps only Shakespeare can impart to his wicked women. Her first appearance and her appeal to Titus is as queenly and noble as anything in the range of dramatic art. . . . We have in Tamora an early study for at least two of

Shakespeare's great women characters—Lady Macbeth and Cleopatra. . . . In Titus we have stray suggestions of no less than three of the great male characters in his acknowledged masterpieces, namely, Lear, Coriolanus, and Hamlet. . . . There are splendid dramatic touches in the treatment of Titus. His sudden laughter, his half-hysterical 'Ha! ha! ha!' for swift and tremendous effect, can, perhaps, only be paralleled by the 'Knocking in Macbeth' for profound and startling dramatic force. . . . The final effect of Titus upon us approximates to that of Lear in being superhuman, titanic, something out of the ordinary scale of humanity; and the same is true, even more so, of Tamora. . . . Lavinia is particularly subtly managed and specially characteristic of Shakespeare . . . she has her successor in Cordelia": and so on to the same effect in a heroic attempt to raise the play from the pit of neglect in which it usually lies. And this attempt culminates in a comparison which is perhaps more illuminating of the methods of some Shakespearean critics than of Titus Andronicus, but which is worth giving if only as a curiosity of criticism. The responsibility for the comparison is shared by Mr Baildon with Mr Crawford, and the comparison is with—of all plays—A Midsummer Night's Dream. As thus:—" In both plays the will of the father is forestalled; Hermia elopes with Lysander, and Lavinia is abducted by Bassianus. The wood and its loneliness play an important part in both dramas, and in both we have the Hunting and the imperial or ducal Marriage. Demetrius quarrels with Lysander, as his namesake with Chiron, and makes a dark threat to Helena, which might mean similar violence to that offered to Lavinia. . . . Some of the leading ideas in the plot are strangely alike, as the marrying a captive queen by Theseus and Saturninus, and the changing of brides in the one, and the criss-cross love-making in the other. Even the sleepy fits of the lovers in the woods cannot fail to remind us of the preternatural drowsiness of the luckless Andronici in *Titus Andronicus*." (Some readers, one hopes, will have no difficulty in failing to be reminded.) . . . "Helena pursuing Demetrius, and Lysander fleeing from Hermia are the reverses of Lavinia pursued by her two brutal lovers. Titania's temporary infatuation for Bottom has its tragic counterpart in Tamora's passion for Aaron." And last, though far from least, Puck appears in the unexpected role of a " comic Aaron." From which flight of fancy, with a famous remark of Puck's in our ears, let us return to sanity with Hazlitt.

" *Titus Andronicus* is certainly as unlike Shakespear's usual style as it is possible. It is an accumulation of vulgar physical horrors, in which the power exercised by the poet bears no proportion to the repugnance excited by the subject. The character of Aaron the Moor is the only thing that shows any originality of conception." And with Schlegel, who, though he finds, and as I am sure one must agree rightly finds, the external evidence for Shakespeare's authorship too strong to be set aside, yet admits that " this tragedy, it is true, is framed according to a false idea of the tragic, which by an accumulation of cruelties and enormities degenerates into the horrible, and yet leaves no deep impression behind."

TITUS ANDRONICUS

DRAMATIS PERSONÆ

SATURNINUS, *son to the late Emperor of Rome, afterwards emperor.*
BASSIANUS, *brother to Saturninus.*
TITUS ANDRONICUS, *a noble Roman.*
MARCUS ANDRONICUS, *tribune of the people, and brother to Titus.*
LUCIUS,
QUINTUS,
MURTIUS, } *sons to Titus Andronicus.*
MUTIUS,
YOUNG LUCIUS, *a boy, son to Lucius.*
PUBLIUS, *son to Marcus Andronicus.*
ÆMILIUS, *a noble Roman.*
ALARBUS,
DEMETRIUS, } *sons to Tamora.*
CHIRON,
AARON, *a Moor, beloved by Tamora.*
A Captain, Tribune, Messenger, and Clown; Romans and Goths.

TAMORA, *Queen of the Goths.*
LAVINIA, *daughter to Titus Andronicus.*
A Nurse, and a black Child.

Kinsmen of Titus, Senators, Tribunes, Officers, Soldiers,
and Attendants.

SCENE : *Rome, and the country near it.*

THE TRAGEDY OF
TITUS ANDRONICUS

Act First

SCENE I

*Rome. Before the Capitol. The Tomb of
the Andronici appearing*

*Flourish. Enter the Tribunes and Senators aloft. And
then enter below, Saturninus and his Followers from one
side, and Bassianus and his Followers from the other
side, with drums and trumpets*

Sat. Noble patricians, patrons of my right,
Defend the justice of my cause with arms.
And, countrymen, my loving followers,
Plead my successive title with your swords :
I am his first-born son, that was the last
That ware the imperial diadem of Rome ;
Then let my father's honours live in me,
Nor wrong mine age with this indignity.

Bas. Romans, friends, followers, favourers of my right,
If ever Bassianus, Cæsar's son,

Were gracious in the eyes of royal Rome,
Keep then this passage to the Capitol,
And suffer not dishonour to approach
The imperial seat, to virtue consecrate,
To justice, continence and nobility :
But let desert in pure election shine,
And, Romans, fight for freedom in your choice.

Enter Marcus Andronicus, aloft, with the crown

Mar. Princes, that strive by factions and by friends
Ambitiously for rule and empery,
Know that the people of Rome, for whom we stand   20
A special party, have by common voice,
In election for the Roman empery,
Chosen Andronicus, surnamed Pius
For many good and great deserts to Rome :
A nobler man, a braver warrior,
Lives not this day within the city walls.
He by the senate is accited home
From weary wars against the barbarous Goths,
That with his sons (a terror to our foes)
Hath yok'd a nation strong, train'd up in arms.   30
Ten years are spent since first he undertook
This cause of Rome, and chastised with arms
Our enemies' pride : five times he hath return'd
Bleeding to Rome, bearing his valiant sons

In coffins from the field.
And now as last, laden with honour's spoils,
Returns the good Andronicus to Rome,
Renowned Titus, flourishing in arms.
Let us entreat, by honour of his name,
Whom worthily you would have now succeed,   40
And in the Capitol and senate's right,
Whom you pretend to honour and adore,
That you withdraw you, and abate your strength,
Dismiss your followers, and, as suitors should,
Plead your deserts in peace and humbleness.

Sat. How fair the tribune speaks to calm my thoughts!

Bas. Marcus Andronicus, so I do affy
In thy uprightness and integrity,
And so I love and honour thee and thine,
Thy noble brother Titus and his sons,   50
And her to whom my thoughts are humbled all,
Gracious Lavinia, Rome's rich ornament,
That I will here dismiss my loving friends;
And to my fortunes and the people's favour
Commit my cause in balance to be weigh'd.

Exeunt the Followers of Bassianus

Sat. Friends, that have been thus forward in my right,
I thank you all, and here dismiss you all,
And to the love and favour of my country

Commit myself, my person and the cause.

Exeunt the Followers of Saturninus

Rome, be as just and gracious unto me,   60

As I am confident and kind to thee.

Open the gates, and let me in.

Bas. Tribunes, and me, a poor competitor.

Flourish.   Saturninus and Bassianus go up into
the Senate-house

Enter a Captain

Cap. Romans, make way : the good Andronicus,

Patron of virtue, Rome's best champion,

Successful in the battles that he fights,

With honour and with fortune is return'd

From where he circumscribed with his sword,

And brought to yoke, the enemies of Rome.

Sound drums and trumpets, and then enter two of Titus' sons, †
and then two men bearing a coffin covered with black, then
two other sons, then Titus Andronicus, and then Tamora
the Queen of Goths and her two sons, Chiron and
Demetrius, with Aaron the Moor and others, as many
as can be, then set down the coffin, and Titus speaks.

Tit. Hail, Rome, victorious in thy mourning weeds !   70

Lo, as the bark that hath discharg'd his fraught

Returns with precious lading to the bay

From whence at first she weigh'd her anchorage,

4

Cometh Andronicus, bound with laurel boughs,
To re-salute his country with his tears,
Tears of true joy for his return to Rome.
Thou great defender of this Capitol,
Stand gracious to the rites that we intend !
Romans, of five and twenty valiant sons,
Half of the number that King Priam had,   80
Behold the poor remains, alive and dead !
These that survive, let Rome reward with love ;
These that I bring unto their latest home,
With burial amongst their ancestors :
Here Goths have given me leave to sheathe my sword.
Titus, unkind, and careless of thine own,
Why suffer'st thou thy sons, unburied yet,
To hover on the dreadful shore of Styx ?
Make way to lay them by their brethren.

They open the tomb

There greet in silence, as the dead are wont,   90
And sleep in peace, slain in your country's wars !
O sacred receptacle of my joys,
Sweet cell of virtue and nobility,
How many sons hast thou of mine in store,
That thou wilt never render to me more !
Luc. Give us the proudest prisoner of the Goths,
That we may hew his limbs and on a pile

    Ad manes fratrum sacrifice his flesh,
    Before this earthy prison of their bones,
    That so the shadows be not unappeas'd,   100
    Nor we disturb'd with prodigies on earth.

Tit. I give him you, the noblest that survives,
    The eldest son of this distressed queen.

Tam. Stay, Roman brethren !   Gracious conqueror,
    Victorious Titus, rue the tears I shed,
    A mother's tears in passion for her son :
    And if thy sons were ever dear to thee,
    O, think my son to be as dear to me !
    Sufficeth not, that we are brought to Rome,
    To beautify thy triumphs, and return   110
    Captive to thee and to thy Roman yoke,
    But must my sons be slaughter'd in the streets,
    For valiant doings in their country's cause ?
    O, if to fight for king and commonweal
    Were piety in thine, it is in these.
    Andronicus, stain not thy tomb with blood.
    Wilt thou draw near the nature of the gods ?
    Draw near them then in being merciful :
    Sweet mercy is nobility's true badge,
    Thrice-noble Titus, spare my first-born son.   120

Tit. Patient yourself, madam, and pardon me.
    These are their brethren, whom you Goths beheld

Alive and dead, and for their brethren slain
Religiously they ask a sacrifice :
To this your son is mark'd, and die he must,
To appease their groaning shadows that are gone.

Luc. Away with him ! and make a fire straight,
And with our swords, upon a pile of wood,
Let 's hew his limbs till they be clean consum'd.

Exeunt the sons of Andronicus with Alarbus

Tam. O cruel, irreligious piety !   130
Chi. Was ever Scythia half so barbarous ?
Dem. Oppose not Scythia to ambitious Rome.
Alarbus goes to rest, and we survive,
To tremble under Titus' threatening look ;
Then, madam, stand resolv'd, but hope withal,
The self-same gods that arm'd the Queen of Troy   †
With opportunity of sharp revenge
Upon the Thracian tyrant in his tent,
May favour Tamora, the queen of Goths,
(When Goths were Goths and Tamora was queen)   140
To quit the bloody wrongs upon her foes.

Re-enter the sons of Andronicus

Luc. See, lord and father, how we have perform'd
Our Roman rites : Alarbus' limbs are lopp'd,
And entrails feed the sacrificing fire,
Whose smoke, like incense, doth perfume the sky.

Remaineth nought but to inter our brethren,
And with loud 'larums welcome them to Rome.

Tit. Let it be so, and let Andronicus
Make this his latest farewell to their souls.

Trumpets sounded, and the coffin laid in the tomb

In peace and honour rest you here, my sons,   150
Rome's readiest champions, repose you here in rest,
Secure from worldly chances and mishaps !
Here lurks no treason, here no envy swells,
Here grow no damned drugs, here are no storms,
No noise, but silence and eternal sleep ;
In peace and honour rest you here, my sons !

Enter Lavinia

Lav. In peace and honour live Lord Titus long ;
My noble lord and father, live in fame !
Lo, at this tomb my tributary tears
I render, for my brethren's obsequies ;   160
And at thy feet I kneel, with tears of joy
Shed on the earth, for thy return to Rome :
O, bless me here with thy victorious hand,
Whose fortunes Rome's best citizens applaud !

Tit. Kind Rome, that hast thus lovingly reserv'd
The cordial of mine age to glad my heart !
Lavinia, live, outlive thy father's days,
And fame's eternal date, for virtue's praise !

Enter, below, Marcus Andronicus and Tribunes ;
re-enter Saturninus and Bassianus, attended

Mar. Long live Lord Titus, my beloved brother,
 Gracious triumpher in the eyes of Rome !   170

Tit. Thanks, gentle tribune, noble brother Marcus.

Mar. And welcome, nephews, from successful wars,
 You that survive, and you that sleep in fame !
 Fair lords, your fortunes are alike in all,
 That in your country's service drew your swords :
 But safer triumph is this funeral pomp,
 That hath aspir'd to Solon's happiness,   †
 And triumphs over chance in honour's bed.
 Titus Andronicus, the people of Rome,
 Whose friend in justice thou hast ever been,   180
 Send thee by me, their tribune and their trust,
 This palliament of white and spotless hue,
 And name thee in election for the empire,
 With these our late-deceased emperor's sons :
 Be candidatus then, and put it on,
 And help to set a head on headless Rome.

Tit. A better head her glorious body fits
 Than his that shakes for age and feebleness :
 What, should I don this robe and trouble you,
 Be chosen with proclamations to-day,   190
 To-morrow yield up rule, resign my life,

9

And set abroad new business for you all?
Rome, I have been thy soldier forty years,
And led my country's strength successfully,
And buried one and twenty valiant sons,
Knighted in field, slain manfully in arms,
In right and service of their noble country:
Give me a staff of honour for mine age,
But not a sceptre to control the world:
Upright he held it, lords, that held it last.   200

Mar. Titus, thou shalt obtain and ask the empery.

Sat. Proud and ambitious tribune, canst thou tell?

Tit. Patience, Prince Saturninus.

Sat.   Romans, do me right;
Patricians, draw your swords, and sheathe them not
Till Saturninus be Rome's emperor.
Andronicus, would thou wert shipp'd to hell,
Rather than rob me of the people's hearts!

Luc. Proud Saturnine, interrupter of the good
That noble-minded Titus means to thee!

Tit. Content thee, prince; I will restore to thee   210
The people's hearts, and wean them from themselves.

Bas. Andronicus, I do not flatter thee,
But honour thee, and will do till I die:
My faction if thou strengthen with thy friends,
I will most thankful be; and thanks to men

Of noble minds is honourable meed.

Tit. People of Rome, and people's tribunes here,
I ask your voices and your suffrages :
Will you bestow them friendly on Andronicus ?

Tribunes. To gratify the good Andronicus,   220
And gratulate his safe return to Rome,
The people will accept whom he admits.

Tit. Tribunes, I thank you : and this suit I make
That you create your emperor's eldest son,
Lord Saturnine, whose virtues will, I hope,
Reflect on Rome as Titan's rays on earth,
And ripen justice in this commonweal :
Then, if you will elect by my advice,
Crown him, and say ' Long live our emperor ! '

Mar. With voices and applause of every sort,   230
Patricians and plebeians, we create
Lord Saturninus Rome's great emperor,
And say ' Long live our Emperor Saturnine !
                         A long flourish till they come down

Sat. Titus Andronicus, for thy favours done
To us in our election this day,
I give thee thanks in part of thy deserts,
And will with deeds requite thy gentleness :
And, for an onset, Titus, to advance
Thy name and honourable family,

Lavinia will I make my emperess, 240
Rome's royal mistress, mistress of my heart,
And in the sacred Pantheon her espouse :
Tell me, Andronicus, doth this motion please thee ?

Tit. It doth, my worthy lord ; and in this match
I hold me highly honour'd of your grace :
And here, in sight of Rome, to Saturnine,
King and commander of our commonweal,
The wide world's emperor, do I consecrate
My sword, my chariot, and my prisoners ;
Presents well worthy Rome's imperious lord : 250
Receive them then, the tribute that I owe,
Mine honour's ensigns humbled at thy feet.

Sat. Thanks, noble Titus, father of my life !
How proud I am of thee and of thy gifts,
Rome shall record ; and when I do forget
The least of these unspeakable deserts,
Romans, forget your fealty to me.

Tit. (*to Tamora*) Now madam, are you prisoner to an
          emperor ;
To him that, for your honour and your state,
Will use you nobly and your followers. 260

Sat. A goodly lady, trust me ; of the hue
That I would choose, were I to choose anew.
Clear up, fair queen, that cloudy countenance :

Though chance of war hath wrought this change of cheer,
Thou com'st not to be made a scorn in Rome :
Princely shall be thy usage every way.
Rest on my word, and let not discontent
Daunt all your hopes : madam, he comforts you
Can make you greater than the Queen of Goths.
Lavinia, you are not displeas'd with this ? 270

Lav. Not I, my lord ; sith true nobility
Warrants these words in princely courtesy.

Sat. Thanks, sweet Lavinia. Romans, let us go :
Ransomless here we set our prisoners free :
Proclaim our honours, lords, with trump and drum.

Bas. Lord Titus, by your leave, this maid is mine.

Tit. How, sir ? are you in earnest then, my lord ?

Bas. Ay, noble Titus, and resolv'd withal
To do myself this reason and this right.

Mar. *Suum cuique* is our Roman justice : 280
This prince in justice seizeth but his own.

Luc. And that he will, and shall, if Lucius live.

Tit. Traitors, avaunt ! Where is the emperor's guard ?
Treason, my lord ! Lavinia is surpris'd !

Sat. Surpris'd ! by whom ?

Bas.   By him that justly may
Bear his betroth'd from all the world away.

Exeunt Bassianus and Marcus with Lavinia

Mut. Brothers, help to convey her hence away,
  And with my sword I'll keep this door safe.
     Exeunt Lucius, Quintus, and Martius

Tit. Follow, my lord, and I'll soon bring her back.

Mut. My lord, you pass not here.

Tit.   What, villain boy!   290
  Barr'st me my way in Rome? *Stabbing Mutius*

Mut.   Help, Lucius, help! *Dies*
   During the fray, Saturninus, Tamora, Demetrius,
    Chiron and Aaron go out, and re-enter above
     Re-enter Lucius

Luc. My lord, you are unjust; and, more than so,
  In wrongful quarrel you have slain your son.

Tit. Nor thou, nor he, are any sons of mine;
  My sons would never so dishonour me:
  Traitor, restore Lavinia to the emperor.

Luc. Dead, if you will; but not to be his wife,
  That is another's lawful promis'd love.   *Exit*

Sat. No, Titus, no; the emperor needs her not,
  Nor her, nor thee, nor any of thy stock: 300
  I'll trust by leisure him that mocks me once;
  Thee never, nor thy traitorous haughty sons,
  Confederates all thus to dishonour me.
  Was none in Rome to make a stale
  But Saturnine? Full well, Andronicus,

   Agree these deeds with that proud brag of thine,
   That saidst, I begg'd the empire at thy hands.

Tit. O monstrous! what reproachful words are these?

Sat. But go thy ways; go give that changing piece
   To him that flourish'd for her with his sword: 310
   A valiant son-in-law thou shalt enjoy;
   One fit to bandy with thy lawless sons,
   To ruffle in the commonwealth of Rome.

Tit. These words are razors to my wounded heart.

Sat. And therefore, lovely Tamora, Queen of Goths,
   That, like the stately Phœbe 'mongst her nymphs,
   Dost overshine the gallant'st dames of Rome,
   If thou be pleas'd with this my sudden choice,
   Behold, I choose thee, Tamora, for my bride,
   And will create thee emperess of Rome.   320
   Speak, Queen of Goths, dost thou applaud my
     choice?
   And here I swear by all the Roman gods,
   Sith priest and holy water are so near,
   And tapers burn so bright, and every thing
   In readiness for Hymenæus stand,
   I will not re-salute the streets of Rome,
   Or climb my palace, till from forth this place
   I lead espous'd my bride along with me.

Tam. And here, in sight of heaven, to Rome I swear,

    If Saturnine advance the Queen of Goths,   330
    She will a handmaid be to his desires,
    A loving nurse, a mother to his youth.

Sat. Ascend, fair queen, Pantheon. Lords, accompany
    Your noble emperor and his lovely bride,
    Sent by the heavens for Prince Saturnine,
    Whose wisdom hath her fortune conquered :
    There shall we consummate our spousal rites.

                          Exeunt all but Titus

Tit. I am not bid to wait upon this bride.
    Titus, when wert thou wont to walk alone,
    Dishonour'd thus and challenged of wrongs ?   340

     Re-enter Marcus, Lucius, Quintus, and Martius

Mar. O Titus, see, O, see what thou hast done !
    In a bad quarrel slain a virtuous son.

Tit. No, foolish tribune, no ; no son of mine,
    Nor thou, nor these, confederates in the deed
    That hath dishonour'd all our family ;
    Unworthy brother, and unworthy sons !

Luc. But let us give him burial, as becomes ;
    Give Mutius burial with our brethren.

Tit. Traitors, away ! he rests not in this tomb :
    This monument five hundred years hath stood,   350
    Which I have sumptuously re-edified :
    Here none but soldiers and Rome's servitors

Repose in fame ; none basely slain in brawls :
Bury him where you can, he comes not here.

Mar. My lord, this is impiety in you :
My nephew Mutius' deeds do plead for him ;
He must be buried with his brethren.

Qui.
Mart. } And shall, or him we will accompany.

Tit. And shall ! what villain was it spake that word ?

Qui. He that would vouch it in any place but here.   360

Tit. What, would you bury him in my despite ?

Mar. No, noble Titus ; but entreat of thee
To pardon Mutius and to bury him.

Tit. Marcus, even thou hast struck upon my crest,
And with these boys mine honour thou hast wounded,
My foes I do repute you every one ;
So trouble me no more, but get you gone.

Mart. He is not with himself ; let us withdraw.

Qui. Not I, till Mutius' bones be buried.

Marcus and the sons of Titus kneel

Mar. Brother, for in that name doth nature plead,—   370

Qui. Father, and in that name doth nature speak,—

Tit. Speak thou no more, if all the rest will speed.

Mar. Renowned Titus, more than half my soul,—

Luc. Dear father, soul and substance of us all,—

Mar. Suffer thy brother Marcus to inter

His noble nephew here in virtue's nest,
That died in honour and Lavinia's cause.
Thou art a Roman; be not barbarous:
The Greeks upon advice did bury Ajax
That slew himself; and wise Laertes' son   †
Did graciously plead for his funerals: 381
Let not young Mutius then, that was thy joy,
Be barr'd his entrance here.

Tit.   Rise, Marcus, rise:
The dismal'st day is this that e'er I saw,
To be dishonour'd by my sons in Rome!
Well, bury him, and bury me the next.

                    Mutius is put into the tomb

Luc. There lie thy bones, sweet Mutius, with thy friends,
Till we with trophies do adorn thy tomb.

All (*kneeling*) No man shed tears for noble Mutius;
He lives in fame that died in virtue's cause.   390

Mar. My lord, to step out of these dreary dumps,
How comes it that the subtle Queen of Goths
Is of a sudden thus advanc'd in Rome?

Tit. I know not, Marcus; but I know it is,
(Whether by device or no, the heavens can tell.)
Is she not then beholding to the man
That brought her for this high good turn so far?
{Yes, and will nobly him remunerate.}

18

Flourish. Re-enter, from one side, Saturninus attended,
Tamora, Demetrius, Chiron, and Aaron ; from the
other, Bassianus, Lavinia, with others

Sat. So, Bassianus, you have play'd your prize :
    God give you joy, sir, of your gallant bride !   400

Bas. And you of yours, my lord ! I say no more,
    Nor wish no less ; and so I take my leave.

Sat. Traitor, if Rome have law, or we have power,
    Thou and thy faction shall repent this rape.

Bas. Rape call you it, my lord, to seize my own,
    My true-betrothed love, and now my wife ?
    But let the laws of Rome determine all ;
    Meanwhile I am possess'd of that is mine.

Sat. 'Tis good, sir : you are very short with us;
    But, if we live, we 'll be as sharp with you.   410

Bas. My lord, what I have done, as best I may,
    Answer I must, and shall do with my life.
    Only thus much I give your grace to know :
    By all the duties that I owe to Rome,
    This noble gentleman, Lord Titus here,
    Is in opinion and in honour wrong'd ;
    That, in the rescue of Lavinia,
    With his own hand did slay his youngest son,
    In zeal to you and highly mov'd to wrath
    To be controll'd in that he frankly gave :   420

Receive him then to favour, Saturnine,
That hath express'd himself in all his deeds
A father and a friend to thee and Rome.

Tit. Prince Bassianus, leave to plead my deeds :
'Tis thou and those that have dishonoured me.
Rome and the righteous heavens be my judge,
How I have lov'd and honour'd Saturnine !

Tam. My worthy lord, if ever Tamora
Were gracious in those princely eyes of thine,
Then hear me speak indifferently for all ;   430
And at my suit, sweet, pardon what is past.

Sat. What, madam ! be dishonoured openly,
And basely put it up without revenge ?

Tam. Not so, my lord ; the gods of Rome forfend
I should be author to dishonour you !
But on mine honour dare I undertake
For good Lord Titus' innocence in all ;
Whose fury not dissembled speaks his griefs :
Then, at my suit, look graciously on him ;
Lose not so noble a friend on vain suppose,   440
Nor with sour looks afflict his gentle heart.
(*aside to Sat.*) My lord, be rul'd by me, be won at last ;
Dissemble all your griefs and discontents :
You are but newly planted in your throne ;
Lest then the people, and patricians too,

Upon a just survey, take Titus' part,
And so supplant you for ingratitude,
Which Rome reputes to be a heinous sin,
Yield at entreats, and then let me alone :
I 'll find a day to massacre them all,   450
And raze their faction and their family,
The cruel father and his traitorous sons,
To whom I sued for my dear son's life ;
And make them know what 'tis to let a queen
Kneel in the streets and beg for grace in vain.—
Come, come, sweet emperor ; come, Andronicus ;
Take up this good old man, and cheer the heart
That dies in tempest of thy angry frown.

Sat. Rise, Titus, rise ; my empress hath prevail'd.

Tit. I thank your majesty, and her, my lord :   460
These words, these looks, infuse new life in me.

Tam. Titus, I am incorporate in Rome,
A Roman now adopted happily,
And must advise the emperor for his good.
This day all quarrels die, Andronicus.
And let it be mine honour, good my lord,
That I have reconcil'd your friends and you.
For you, Prince Bassianus, I have pass'd
My word and promise to the emperor,
That you will be more mild and tractable.   470

> And fear not, lords, and you, Lavinia ;
> By my advice, all humbled on your knees
> You shall ask pardon of his majesty.

Luc. We do ; and vow to heaven, and to his highness,
> That what we did was mildly as we might,
> Tendering our sister's honour and our own.

Mar. That, on mine honour, here I do protest.

Sat. Away, and talk not ; trouble us no more.

Tam. Nay, nay, sweet emperor, we must all be friends :
> The tribune and his nephews kneel for grace ;   480
> I will not be denied : sweet heart, look back.

Sat. Marcus, for thy sake and thy brother's here,
> And at my lovely Tamora's entreats,
> I do remit these young men's heinous faults :
> Stand up.
> Lavinia, though you left me like a churl,
> I found a friend ; and sure as death I swore
> I would not part a bachelor from the priest.
> Come, if the emperor's court can feast two brides,
> You are my guest, Lavinia, and your friends.   490
> This day shall be a love-day, Tamora.

Tit. To-morrow, an it please your majesty
> To hunt the panther and the hart with me,
> With horn and hound we 'll give your grace bonjour.

Sat. Be it so, Titus, and gramercy too.   *Flourish.   Exeunt*

Act Second

SCENE I

Rome. Before the palace

Enter Aaron

*Aar.*Now climbeth Tamora Olympus' top,
   Safe out of fortune's shot, and sits aloft,
   Secure of thunder's crack or lightning flash,
   Advanc'd above pale envy's threatening reach.
   As when the golden sun salutes the morn,
   And, having gilt the ocean with his beams,
   Gallops the zodiac in his glistering coach,
   And overlooks the highest-peering hills ;
   So Tamora :
   Upon her wit doth earthly honour wait,   10
   And virtue stoops and trembles at her frown.
   Then, Aaron, arm thy heart, and fit thy thoughts,
   To mount aloft with thy imperial mistress,
   And mount her pitch, whom thou in triumph long
   Hast prisoner held, fetter'd in amorous chains,
   And faster bound to Aaron's charming eyes
   Than is Prometheus tied to Caucasus.   †
   Away with slavish weeds and servile thoughts !

I will be bright, and shine in pearl and gold,
To wait upon this new-made emperess.   20
To wait, said I ? to wanton with this queen,
This goddess, this Semiramis, this nymph,
This siren, that will charm Rome's Saturnine,
And see his shipwreck and his commonweal's.
Holloa ! what storm is this ?

Enter Demetrius and Chiron, braving

*Dem.*Chiron, thy years want wit, thy wit wants edge
And manners, to intrude where I am grac'd,
And may, for aught thou know'st, affected be.

Chi. Demetrius, thou dost over-ween in all,
And so in this, to bear me down with braves.   30
'Tis not the difference of a year or two
Makes me less gracious, or thee more fortunate :
I am as able and as fit as thou
To serve, and to deserve my mistress' grace ;
And that my sword upon thee shall approve,
And plead my passions for Lavinia's love.

Aar.(aside) Clubs, clubs ! these lovers will not keep the
          peace.

*Dem.*Why, boy, although our mother, unadvis'd,
Gave you a dancing-rapier by your side,
Are you so desperate grown, to threat your friends ?   40
Go to ; have your lath glued within your sheath

Till you know better how to handle it.

Chi. Meanwhile, sir, with the little skill I have,
Full well shalt thou perceive how much I dare.

Dem. Ay, boy, grow ye so brave ?   *They draw*

Aar.(*coming forward*)   Why, how now, lords !
So near the emperor's palace dare you draw,
And maintain such a quarrel openly ?
Full well I wot the ground of all this grudge :
I would not for a million of gold
The cause were known to them it most concerns,   50
Nor would your noble mother for much more
Be so dishonoured in the court of Rome.
For shame, put up.

Dem.   Not I, till I have sheath'd
My rapier in his bosom, and withal
Thrust those reproachful speeches down his throat,
That he hath breath'd in my dishonour here.

Chi. For that I am prepar'd and full resolv'd.
Foul-spoken coward ! that thundrest with thy tongue,
And with thy weapon nothing dar'st perform.

*Aar.*Away, I say !   60
Now, by the gods that warlike Goths adore,
This petty brabble will undo us all.
Why, lords, and think you not how dangerous
It is to jet upon a prince's right ?

What, is Lavinia then become so loose,
Or Bassianus so degenerate,
That for her love such quarrels may be broach'd
Without controlment, justice, or revenge?
Young lords, beware! an should the empress know
This discord's ground, the music would not please. 70

Chi. I care not, I, knew she and all the world:
I love Lavinia more than all the world.

Dem. Youngling, learn thou to make some meaner choice:
Lavinia is thine elder brother's hope.

Aar. Why, are ye mad? or know ye not, in Rome
How furious and impatient they be,
And cannot brook competitors in love?
I tell you, lords, you do but plot your deaths
By this device.

Chi.   Aaron, a thousand deaths
Would I propose to achieve her whom I love. 80

Aar. To achieve her! how?

Dem.   Why mak'st thou it so strange?
She is a woman, therefore may be woo'd;
She is a woman, therefore may be won;
She is Lavinia, therefore must be lov'd.
What, man! more water glideth by the mill
Than wots the miller of; and easy it is
Of a cut loaf to steal a shive, we know:

Though Bassianus be the emperor's brother,
Better than he have worn Vulcan's badge.

Aar.(aside) Ay, and as good as Saturninus may.   90

Dem. Then why should he despair that knows to court it
With words, fair looks, and liberality ?
What, hast not thou full often struck a doe,
And borne her cleanly by the keeper's nose ?

Aar. Why, then, it seems, some certain snatch or so
Would serve your turns.

Chi.   Ay, so the turn were serv'd.

Dem. Aaron, thou hast hit it.

Aar.   Would you had hit it too !
Then should not we be tir'd with this ado.
Why, hark ye, hark ye ! and are you such fools
To square for this ? would it offend you, then,   100
[That both should speed ?]

Chi. Faith, not me.

Dem.   Nor me, so I were one.

Aar. For shame, be friends, and join for that you jar :
'Tis policy and stratagem must do
That you affect ; and so must you resolve,
That what you cannot as you would achieve,
You must perforce accomplish as you may.
Take this of me : Lucrece was not more chaste   †
Than this Lavinia, Bassianus' love.

A speedier **course** than lingering languishment   110
Must we pursue, and I have found the path.
My lords, a solemn hunting is in hand ;
There will the lovely Roman ladies troop :
The forest walks are wide and spacious ;
And many unfrequented plots there are
Fitted by kind for rape and villany :
Single you thither then this dainty doe,
And strike her home by force, if not by words :
This way, or not at all, stand you in hope.
Come, come, our empress, with her sacred wit   120
To villany and vengeance consecrate,
Will we **acquaint** with all that we intend ;
And she shall file our engines with advice,
That will not suffer you to square yourselves,
But to your wishes' height advance you both.
The emperor's court is like the house of Fame,
The palace full of tongues, of eyes and ears :
The woods are ruthless, dreadful, deaf and dull ;
There speak, and strike, brave boys, and take your
    turns ;
There serve your lust, shadow'd from heaven's eye, 130
And revel in Lavinia's treasury.

Chi. Thy counsel, lad, smells of no cowardice.

Dem.Sit fas aut nefas, till I find the stream   †

To cool this heat, a charm to calm these fits,

Per Styga, per manes vehor.　　　　　*Exeunt*

SCENE II

A forest near Rome.　Horns and cry of hounds heard

*Enter Titus Andronicus, with Hunters, &c., Marcus,
Lucius, Quintus, and Martius*

Tit. The hunt is up, the morn is bright and grey,
　　The fields are fragrant, and the woods are green :
　　Uncouple here, and let us make a bay,
　　And wake the emperor and his lovely bride,
　　And rouse the prince, and ring a hunter's peal,
　　That all the court may echo with the noise,
　　Sons, let it be your charge, as it is ours,
　　To attend the emperor's person carefully.
　　I have been troubled in my sleep this night,
　　But dawning day new comfort hath inspir'd.　　10

*A cry of hounds, and horns winded in a peal.　Enter Saturninus,
Tamora, Bassianus, Lavinia, Demetrius, Chiron, and
their Attendants*

　　Many good morrows to your majesty ;
　　Madam, to you as many and as good :
　　I promised your grace a hunter's peal.

Sat. And you have rung it lustily, my lords ;
    Somewhat too early for new-married ladies.

Bas. Lavinia, how say you ?

Lav.   I say, no ;
    I have been broad awake two hours and more.

Sat. Come on then ; horse and chariots let us have,
    And to our sport.   (*to Tamora*) Madam, now shall
      ye see
    Our Roman hunting.

Mar.   I have dogs, my lord,   20
    Will rouse the proudest panther in the chase,
    And climb the highest promontory top.

Tit. And I have horse will follow where the game
    Makes way, and runs like swallows o'er the plain.

Dem. Chiron, we hunt not, we, with horse nor hound,
    But hope to pluck a dainty doe to ground.   *Exeunt*

SCENE III

A lonely part of the forest

Enter Aaron, with a bag of gold

Aar. He that had wit would think that I had none,
    To bury so much gold under a tree.
    And never after to inherit it.

Let him that thinks of me so abjectly
Know that this gold must coin a stratagem,
Which, cunningly effected, will beget
A very excellent piece of villany :
And so repose, sweet gold, for their unrest
That have their alms out of the empress' chest.

Hides the gold

Enter Tamora

*Tam.*My lovely Aaron, wherefore look'st thou sad,   10
When every thing doth make a gleeful boast ?
The birds chant melody on every bush ;
The snake lies rolled in the cheerful sun ;
The green leaves quiver with the cooling wind,
And make a chequer'd shadow on the ground :
Under their sweet shade, Aaron, let us sit,
And, whilst the babbling echo mocks the hounds,
Replying shrilly to the well-tun'd horns,
As if a double hunt were heard at once,
Let us sit down and mark their yellowing noise ;   20
And, after conflict such as was suppos'd
The wandering prince and Dido once enjoy'd,   †
When with a happy storm they were surpris'd,
And curtain'd with a counsel-keeping cave,
We may, each wreathed in the other's arms,
(Our pastimes done) possess a golden slumber ;

31

Whiles hounds and horns and sweet melodious birds
Be unto us as is a nurse's song
Of lullaby to bring her babe asleep.

*Aar.*Madam, though Venus govern your desires,⁣   30
Saturn is dominator over mine :
What signifies my deadly-standing eye,
My silence and my cloudy melancholy,
My fleece of woolly hair that now uncurls
Even as an adder when she doth unroll
To do some fatal execution ?
No, madam, these are no venereal signs :
Vengeance is in my heart, death in my hand,
Blood and revenge are hammering in my head.
Hark, Tamora, the empress of my soul,⁣   40
Which never hopes more heaven than rests in thee,
This is the day of doom for Bassianus :
His Philomel must lose her tongue to-day,⁣   †
Thy sons make pillage of her chastity,
And wash their hands in Bassianus' blood.
Seest thou this letter ? take it up, I pray thee,
And give the king this fatal-plotted scroll.
Now question me no more ; we are espied ;
Here comes a parcel of our hopeful booty,
Which dreads not yet their lives' destruction.⁣   50

*Tam.*Ah, my sweet Moor, sweeter to me than life !

Aar. No more, great empress ; Bassianus comes :
　　Be cross with him, and I 'll go fetch thy sons
　　To back thy quarrels, whatsoe'er they be.　　*Exit*
　　　　　Enter Bassianus and Lavinia

Bas. Who have we here ?　Rome's royal emperess,
　　Unfurnish'd of her well-beseeming troop ?
　　Or is it Dian, habited like her,
　　Who hath abandoned her holy groves
　　To see the general hunting in this forest ?

Tam. Saucy controller of my private steps !　　　　　60
　　Had I the power that some say Dian had,
　　Thy temples should be planted presently
　　With horns, as was Actæon's, and the hounds　　†
　　Should drive upon thy new-transformed limbs,
　　Unmannerly intruder as thou art !

Lav. Under your patience, gentle empress,
　　'Tis thought you have a goodly gift in horning ;
　　And to be doubted that your Moor and you
　　Are singled forth to try experiments :
　　Jove shield your husband from his hounds to-day !　70
　　'Tis pity they should take him for a stag.

Bas. Believe me, queen, your swarty Cimmerian
　　Doth make your honour of his body's hue,
　　Spotted, detested, and abominable.
　　Why are you sequester'd from all your train,

Dismounted from your snow-white goodly steed,
And wander'd hither to an obscure plot,
Accompanied but with a barbarous Moor,
If foul desire had not conducted you?

Lav. And, being intercepted in your sport, 80
Great reason that my noble lord be rated
For sauciness. I pray you, let us hence,
And let her joy her raven-coloured love;
This valley fits the purpose passing well.

Bas. The king my brother shall have notice of this.

Lav. Ay, for these slips have made him noted long:
Good king, to be so mightily abus'd!

Tam. Why, I have patience to endure all this.

Enter Demetrius and Chiron

Dem. How now, dear sovereign, and our gracious mother?
Why doth your highness look so pale and wan? 90

Tam. Have I not reason, think you, to look pale?
These two have tic'd me hither to this place:
A barren detested vale you see it is;
The trees, though summer, yet forlorn and lean,
O'ercome with moss and baleful mistletoe:
Here never shines the sun; here nothing breeds,
Unless the nightly owl or fatal raven:
And when they show'd me this abhorred pit,
They told me, here, at dead time of the night,

34

A thousand fiends, a thousand hissing snakes, 100
Ten thousand swelling toads, as many urchins,
Would make such fearful and confused cries,
As any mortal body hearing it
Should straight fall mad, or else die suddenly.
No sooner had they told this hellish tale,
But straight they told me they would bind me here
Unto the body of a dismal yew,
And leave me to this miserable death :
And then they call'd me foul adulteress,
Lascivious Goth, and all the bitterest terms 110
That ever ear did hear to such effect :
And, had you not by wondrous fortune come,
This vengeance on me had they executed.
Revenge it, as you love your mother's life,
Or be ye not henceforth call'd my children.

*Dem.*This is a witness that I am thy son.

> *Stabs Bassianus*

Chi. And this for me, struck home to show my strength.

> *Also stabs Bassianus, who dies*

Lav. Ay, come, Semiramis, nay, barbarous Tamora,
　　For no name fits thy nature but thy own !

*Tam.*Give me the poniard ; you shall know, my boys, 120
　　Your mother's hand shall right your mother's wrong.

*Dem.*Stay, madam ; here is more belongs to her ;

²d

35

First thrash the corn, then after burn the straw ;
This minion stood upon her chastity,
Upon her nuptial vow, her loyalty,
And with that painted hope braves your mightiness :
And shall she carry this unto her grave ?

Chi. An if she do, I would I were an eunuch.
Drag hence her husband to some secret hole,
And make his dead trunk pillow to our lust.   130

Tam. But when ye have the honey we desire,
Let not this wasp outlive us both to sting.

Chi. I warrant you, madam, we will make that sure.
Come, mistress, now perforce we will enjoy
That nice-preserved honesty of yours.

Lav. O Tamora ! thou bear'st a woman's face—

Tam. I will not hear her speak ; away with her !

Lav. Sweet lords, entreat her hear me but a word.

Dem. Listen, fair madam : let it be your glory
To see her tears, but be your heart to them   140
As unrelenting flint to drops of rain.

Lav. When did the tiger's young ones teach the dam ?
O, do not learn her wrath ; she taught it thee ;
The milk thou suck'dst from her did turn to marble ;
Even at thy teat thou hadst thy tyranny.
Yet every mother breeds not sons alike :
(*to Chiron*) Do thou entreat her show a woman pity.

Chi. What, wouldst thou have me prove myself a bastard?

Lav. 'Tis true the raven doth not hatch a lark:
  Yet have I heard,—O, could I find it now!—   150
  The lion, moved with pity, did endure
  To have his princely paws par'd all away:
  Some say that ravens foster forlorn children,
  The whilst their own birds famish in their nests:
  O, be to me, though thy hard heart say no,
  Nothing so kind, but something pitiful!

Tam. I know not what it means: away with her!

Lav. O, let me teach thee for my father's sake,
  That gave thee life, when well he might have slain thee,
  Be not obdurate, open thy deaf ears.   160

Tam. Hadst thou in person ne'er offended me,
  Even for his sake am I pitiless.
  Remember, boys, I pour'd forth tears in vain
  To save your brother from the sacrifice;
  But fierce Andronicus would not relent:
  Therefore, away with her, and use her as you will;
  The worse to her, the better lov'd of me.

Lav. O Tamora, be call'd a gentle queen,
  And with thine own hands kill me in this place!
  For 'tis not life that I have begg'd so long;   170
  Poor I was slain when Bassianus died.

Tam. What begg'st thou then? fond woman, let me go.

Lav. 'Tis present death I beg ; and one thing more
That womanhood denies my tongue to tell :
O, keep me from their worse than killing lust,
And tumble me into some loathsome pit,
Where never man's eye may behold my body :
Do this, and be a charitable murderer.

Tam. So should I rob my sweet sons of their fee :
No, let them satisfy their lust on thee.   180

Dem. Away ! for thou hast stay'd us here too long.

Lav. No grace ? no womanhood ?   Ah, beastly creature !
The blot and enemy to our general name !
Confusion fall—

Chi. Nay, then I 'll stop your mouth.   Bring thou her
     husband :
This is the hole where Aaron bid us hide him.

> *Demetrius throws the body of Bassianus into the
>   pit ; then exeunt Demetrius and Chiron,
>   dragging off Lavinia*

Tam. Farewell, my sons ; see that you make her sure.
Ne'er let my heart know merry cheer indeed,
Till all the Andronici be made away.
Now will I hence to seek my lovely Moor,   190
And let my spleenful sons this trull deflower.   *Exit*

> *Re-enter Aaron, with Quintus and Martius*

Aar. Come on, my lords, the better foot before :

Straight will I bring you to the loathsome pit
Where I espied the panther fast asleep.

Qui. My sight is very dull, whate'er it bodes.

Mar. And mine, I promise you ; were it not for shame,
Well could I leave our sport to sleep awhile.

Falls into the pit

Qui. What, art thou fall'n ?   What subtle hole is this,
Whose mouth is cover'd with rude-growing briers,
Upon whose leaves are drops of new-shed blood   200
As fresh as morning dew distill'd on flowers ?
A very fatal place it seems to me.
Speak, brother, hast thou hurt thee with the fall ?

Mar. O brother, with the dismal'st object hurt
That ever eye with sight made heart lament !

Aar. (*aside*) Now will I fetch the king to find them here,
That he thereby may have a likely guess
How these were they that made away his brother.

Exit

Mar. Why dost not comfort me, and help me out
From this unhallow'd and blood-stained hole ?   210

Qui. I am surprised with an uncouth fear,
A chilling sweat o'er-runs my trembling joints,
My heart suspects more than mine eye can see.

Mar. To prove thou hast a true-divining heart,
Aaron and thou look down into this den,

39

And see a fearful sight of blood and death.

Qui. Aaron is gone, and my compassionate heart
    Will not permit mine eyes once to behold
    The thing whereat it trembles by surmise:
    O, tell me who it is, for ne'er till now   220
    Was I a child to fear I know not what.

Mar. Lord Bassianus lies embrewed here,
    All on a heap, like to a slaughter'd lamb,
    In this detested, dark, blood-drinking pit.

Qui. If it be dark, how dost thou know 'tis he?

Mar. Upon his bloody finger he doth wear
    A precious ring, that lightens all this hole,
    Which, like a taper in some monument,
    Doth shine upon the dead man's earthy cheeks,
    And shows the ragged entrails of this pit: 230
    So pale did shine the moon on Pyramus   †
    When he by night lay bath'd in maiden blood.
    O brother, help me with thy fainting hand—
    If fear hath made thee faint, as me it hath—
    Out of this fell devouring receptacle,
    As hateful as Cocytus' misty mouth.

Qui. Reach me thy hand, that I may help thee out;
    Or, wanting strength to do thee so much good,
    I may be pluck'd into the swallowing womb
    Of this deep pit, poor Bassianus' grave.   240

I have no strength to pluck thee to the brink.

Mar. Nor I no strength to climb without thy help.

Qui. Thy hand once more ; I will not loose again,
Till thou art here aloft, or I below :
Thou canst not come to me : I come to thee.

Falls in

Enter Saturninus with Aaron

Sat. Along with me : I 'll see what hole is here,
And what he is that now is leap'd into it.
Say, who art thou that lately didst descend
Into this gaping hollow of the earth ?

Mar. The unhappy son of old Andronicus ;   250
Brought hither in a most unlucky hour,
To find thy brother Bassianus dead.

Sat. My brother dead ? I know thou dost but jest :
He and his lady both are at the lodge
Upon the north side of this pleasant chase ;
'Tis not an hour since I left them there.

Mar. We know not where you left them all alive ;
But, out, alas ! here have we found him dead.

*Re-enter Tamora, with Attendants ; Titus Andronicus,
and Lucius*

Tam. Where is my lord the king ?

Sat. Here, Tamora ; though griev'd with killing grief.   260

Tam. Where is thy brother Bassianus ?

Sat. Now to the bottom dost thou search my wound :
   Poor Bassianus here lies murdered.

Tam. Then all too late I bring this fatal writ,
   The complot of this timeless tragedy ;
   And wonder greatly that man's face can fold
   In pleasing smiles such murderous tyranny.

She gives a letter

Sat. (*reads*) ' An if we miss to meet him handsomely—
   Sweet huntsman, Bassianus 'tis we mean—
   Do thou so much as dig the grave for him :   270
   Thou know'st our meaning.   Look for thy reward
   Among the nettles at the elder-tree,
   Which overshades the mouth of that same pit
   Where we decreed to bury Bassianus.
   Do this and purchase us thy lasting friends.'
   O Tamora ! was ever heard the like ?
   This is the pit, and this the elder-tree.
   Look, sirs, if you can find the huntsman out
   That should have murder'd Bassianus here.

Aar. My gracious lord, here is the bag of gold.   280

Sat. (*to Titus*) Two of thy whelps, fell curs of bloody kind,
   Have here bereft my brother of his life.
   Sirs, drag them from the pit unto the prison :
   There let them bide until we have devis'd
   Some never-heard-of torturing pain for them.

*Tam.*What, are they in this pit ?   O wondrous thing !
　　How easily murder is discovered !

Tit. High emperor, upon my feeble knee
　　I beg this boon, with tears not lightly shed,
　　That this fell fault of my accursed sons,　　　　290
　　Accursed, if the fault be prov'd in them—

Sat. If it be prov'd ? you see it is apparent.
　　Who found this letter ?   Tamora, was it you ?

*Tam.*Andronicus himself did take it up.

Tit. I did, my lord : yet let me be their bail ;
　　For, by my fathers' reverend tomb, I vow
　　They shall be ready at your highness' will,
　　To answer their suspicion with their lives.

Sat. Thou shalt not bail them : see thou follow me.
　　Some bring the murder'd body, some the murderers :　300
　　Let them not speak a word ; the guilt is plain ;
　　For, by my soul, were there worse end than death,
　　That end upon them should be executed.

*Tam.*Andronicus, I will entreat the king :
　　Fear not thy sons ; they shall do well enough.

Tit. Come, Lucius, come : stay not to talk with them.

　　　　　　　　　　　　　　　Exeunt

SCENE IV

Another part of the forest

*Enter Demetrius and Chiron, with Lavinia, her hands
cut off, and her tongue cut out, and ravished*

Dem. So, now go tell, an if thy tongue can speak,
  Who 'twas that cut thy tongue and ravish'd thee.
Chi. Write down thy mind, bewray thy meaning so,
  An if thy stumps will let thee play the scribe.
Dem. See, how with signs and tokens she can scrowl.
Chi. Go home, call for sweet water, wash thy hands.
Dem. She hath no tongue to call, nor hands to wash ;
  And so let 's leave her to her silent walks.
Chi. An 'twere my cause, I should go hang myself.
Dem. If thou hadst hands to help thee knit the cord. 10

Exeunt Demetrius and Chiron

Enter Marcus, from hunting

Mar. Who is this ? my niece, that flies away so fast ?
  Cousin, a word ; where is your husband ?
  If I do dream, would all my wealth would wake me !
  If I do wake, some planet strike me down,
  That I may slumber in eternal sleep !
  Speak, gentle niece, what stern ungentle hands
  Have lopp'd, and hew'd, and made thy body bare
  Of her two branches, those sweet ornaments,

Whose circling shadows kings have sought to sleep in,
And might not gain so great a happiness   20
As half thy love?   Why dost not speak to me?
Alas, a crimson river of warm blood,
Like to a bubbling fountain stirr'd with wind,
Doth rise and fall between thy rosed lips,
Coming and going with thy honey breath.
But, sure, some Tereus hath deflowered thee,   †
And, lest thou shouldst detect him, cut thy tongue.
Ah, now thou turn'st away thy face for shame!
And, notwithstanding all this loss of blood,
As from a conduit with three issuing spouts,   30
Yet do thy cheeks look red as Titan's face
Blushing to be encounter'd with a cloud.
Shall I speak for thee? shall I say 'tis so?
O, that I knew thy heart; and knew the beast,
That I might rail at him, to ease my mind!
Sorrow concealed, like an oven stopp'd,
Doth burn the heart to cinders where it is.
Fair Philomel, why she but lost her tongue,
And in a tedious sampler sew'd her mind:
But, lovely niece, that mean is cut from thee;   40
A craftier Tereus, cousin, hast thou met,
And he hath cut those pretty fingers off,
That could have better sew'd than Philomel.

45

O, had the monster seen those lily hands
Tremble, like aspen-leaves, upon a lute,
And make the silken strings delight to kiss them,
He would not then have touch'd them for his life !
Or, had he heard the heavenly harmony
Which that sweet tongue hath made,
He would have dropp'd his knife, and fell asleep   50
As Cerberus at the Thracian poet's feet.   †
Come, let us go and make thy father blind ;
For such a sight will blind a father's eye :
One hour's storm will drown the fragrant meads ;
What will whole months of tears thy father's eyes ?
Do not draw back, for we will mourn with thee :
O, could our mourning ease thy misery !   *Exeunt*

Act Third

SCENE I

Rome.   A street

Enter Judges, Senators, and Tribunes, with Martius and
Quintus, bound, passing on the stage to the place of execu-
tion, and Titus going before, pleading

Tit. Hear me, grave fathers ! noble tribunes, stay !
For pity of mine age, whose youth was spent
In dangerous wars, whilst you securely slept.
For all my blood in Rome's great quarrel shed,
For all the frosty nights that I have watch'd,
And for these bitter tears, which now you see,
Filling the aged wrinkles in my cheeks ;
Be pitiful to my condemned sons,
Whose souls are not corrupted as 'tis thought.
For two and twenty sons I never wept,   **10**
Because they died in honour's lofty bed.

  Lieth down ; the Judges, &c. pass by him, and Exeunt
For these, tribunes, in the dust I write
My heart's deep languor and my soul's sad tears :
Let my tears stanch the earth's dry appetite ;
My sons' sweet blood will make it shame and blush :

O earth, I will befriend thee more with rain,
That shall distil from these two ancient urns, †
Than youthful April shall with all his showers :
In summer's drought I'll drop upon thee still ;
In winter with warm tears I'll melt the snow, 20
And keep eternal spring-time on thy face,
So thou refuse to drink my dear sons' blood.

Enter Lucius, with his weapon drawn

O reverend tribunes ! O gentle, aged men !
Unbind my sons, reverse the doom of death ;
And let me say, that never wept before,
My tears are now prevailing orators.

Luc. O noble father, you lament in vain :
The tribunes hear you not ; no man is by ;
And you recount your sorrows to a stone.

Tit. Ah, Lucius, for thy brothers let me plead. 30
Grave tribunes, once more I entreat of you,—

Luc. My gracious lord, no tribune hears you speak.

Tit. Why, 'tis no matter, man : if they did hear,
They would not mark me ; or if they did mark, †
They would not pity me ; yet plead I must,
And bootless unto them . . . . . .
Therefore I tell my sorrows to the stones ;
Who, though they cannot answer my distress,
Yet in some sort they are better than the tribunes,

For that they will not intercept my tale :   40
When I do weep, they humbly at my feet
Receive my tears, and seem to weep with me ;
And, were they but attired in grave weeds,
Rome could afford no tribune like to these.
A stone is soft as wax, tribunes more hard than stones ;
A stone is silent and offendeth not,
And tribunes with their tongues doom men to death.

Rises

But wherefore stand'st thou with thy weapon drawn ?

Luc. To rescue my two brothers from their death :
For which attempt the judges have pronounc'd   50
My everlasting doom of banishment.

Tit. O happy man ! they have befriended thee.
Why, foolish Lucius, dost thou not perceive
That Rome is but a wilderness of tigers ?
Tigers must prey, and Rome affords no prey
But me and mine : how happy art thou then,
From these devourers to be banished !
But who comes with our brother Marcus here ?

Enter Marcus and Lavinia

Mar. Titus, prepare thy aged eyes to weep ;
Or, if not so, thy noble heart to break :   60
I bring consuming sorrow to thine age.

Tit. Will it consume me ? let me see it then.

49

Mar. This was thy daughter.

Tit.   Why, Marcus, so she is.

Luc. Ay me, this object kills me !

Tit. Faint-hearted boy, arise, and look upon her.
    Speak, Lavinia, what accursed hand
    Hath made thee handless in thy father's sight ?
    What fool hath added water to the sea,
    Or brought a faggot to bright-burning Troy ?
    My grief was at the height before thou cam'st ;   70
    And now, like Nilus, it disdaineth bounds.
    Give me a sword, I'll chop off my hands too ;
    For they have fought for Rome, and all in vain ;
    And they have nurs'd this woe, in feeding life ;
    In bootless prayer have they been held up,
    And they have serv'd me to effectless use :
    Now all the service I require of them
    Is, that the one will help to cut the other.
    'Tis well, Lavinia, that thou hast no hands ;
    For hands to do Rome service is but vain.   80

Luc. Speak, gentle sister, who hath martyr'd thee ?

Mar. O, that delightful engine of her thoughts,
    That blabb'd them with such pleasing eloquence,
    Is torn from forth that pretty hollow cage,
    Where, like a sweet melodious bird, it sung
    Sweet varied notes, enchanting every ear !

Luc. O, say thou for her, who hath done this deed?

Mar. O, thus I found her, straying in the park,
  Seeking to hide herself, as doth the deer
  That hath received some unrecuring wound.   90

Tit. It was my dear; and he that wounded her
  Hath hurt me more than had he kill'd me dead:
  For now I stand as one upon a rock,
  Environ'd with a wilderness of sea;
  Who marks the waxing tide grow wave by wave,
  Expecting ever when some envious surge
  Will in his brinish bowels swallow him.
  This way to death my wretched sons are gone,
  Here stands my other son, a banish'd man,
  And here my brother, weeping at my woes: 100
  But that which gives my soul the greatest spurn,
  Is dear Lavinia, dearer than my soul.
  Had I but seen thy picture in this plight,
  It would have madded me: what shall I do,
  Now I behold thy lively body so?
  Thou hast no hands, to wipe away thy tears,
  Nor tongue, to tell me who hath martyr'd thee:
  Thy husband he is dead, and for his death
  Thy brothers are condemn'd, and dead by this.
  Look, Marcus, ah, son Lucius, look on her!   110
  When I did name her brothers, then fresh tears

       Stood on her cheeks, as doth the honey-dew
       Upon a gather'd lily almost wither'd

Mar. Perchance she weeps because they kill'd her husband,
       Perchance because she knows them innocent.

Tit. If they did kill thy husband, then be joyful,
       Because the law hath ta'en revenge on them.
       No, no, they would not do so foul a deed ;
       Witness the sorrow that their sister makes.
       Gentle Lavinia, let me kiss thy lips ;   120
       Or make some sign how I may do thee ease :
       Shall thy good uncle, and thy brother Lucius,
       And thou, and I, sit round about some fountain,
       Looking all downwards, to behold our cheeks
       How they are stain'd, as meadows yet not dry
       With miry slime left on them by a flood ?
       And in the fountain shall we gaze so long,
       Till the fresh taste be taken from that clearness,
       And made a brine-pit with our bitter tears ?
       Or shall we cut away our hands, like thine ?   130
       Or shall we bite our tongues, and in dumb shows
       Pass the remainder of our hateful days ?
       What shall we do ? let us, that have our tongues,
       Plot some device of further misery,
       To make us wonder'd at in time to come.

Luc. Sweet father, cease your tears ; for, at your grief,

See how my wretched sister sobs and weeps.

Mar. Patience, dear niece.   Good Titus, dry thine eyes.

Tit. Ah, Marcus, Marcus! brother, well I wot
    Thy napkin cannot drink a tear of mine,   140
    For thou, poor man, hast drown'd it with thine own.

Luc. Ah, my Lavinia, I will wipe thy cheeks.

Tit. Mark, Marcus, mark! I understand her signs:
    Had she a tongue to speak, now would she say
    That to her brother which I said to thee:
    His napkin, with his true tears all bewet,
    Can do no service on her sorrowful cheeks.
    O, what a sympathy of woe is this,
    As far from help as Limbo is from bliss!

Enter Aaron

Aar. Titus Andronicus, my lord the emperor   150
    Sends thee this word, that, if thou love thy sons,
    Let Marcus, Lucius, or thyself, old Titus,
    Or any one of you, chop off your hand,
    And send it to the king: he for the same
    Will send thee hither both thy sons alive;
    And that shall be the ransom for their fault.

Tit. O gracious emperor! O gentle Aaron!
    Did ever raven sing so like a lark,
    That gives sweet tidings of the sun's uprise?
    With all my heart, I'll send the emperor   160

My hand :
Good Aaron, wilt thou help to chop it off ?
Luc. Stay, father ! for that noble hand of thine,
That hath thrown down so many enemies,
Shall not be sent : my hand will serve the turn :
My youth can better spare my blood than you ;
And therefore mine shall save my brothers' lives.
Mar. Which of your hands hath not defended Rome,
And rear'd aloft the bloody battle-axe,
Writing destruction on the enemy's castle :   †
O, none of both but are of high desert :   171
My hand hath been but idle ; let it serve
To ransom my two nephews from their death ;
Then have I kept it to a worthy end.
Aar. Nay, come, agree whose hand shall go along,
For fear they die before their pardon come.
Mar. My hand shall go.
Luc.   By heaven, it shall not go !
Tit. Sirs, strive no more : such wither'd herbs as these
Are meet for plucking up, and therefore mine.
Luc. Sweet father, if I shall be thought thy son,   180
Let me redeem my brothers both from death.
Mar. And, for our father's sake and mother's care,
Now let me show a brother's love to thee.
Tit. Agree between you ; I will spare my hand.

Luc. Then I 'll go fetch an axe.

Mar. But I will use the axe.   *Exeunt Lucius and Marcus*

Tit. Come hither, Aaron ; I 'll deceive them both :
    Lend me thy hand, and I will give thee mine.

Aar. (*aside*) If that be call'd deceit, I will be honest,
    And never, whilst I live, deceive men so :   190
    But I 'll deceive you in another sort,
    And that you 'll say, ere half an hour pass.

                   Cuts off Titus's hand

          Re-enter Lucius and Marcus

Tit. Now stay your strife : what shall be is dispatch'd.
    Good Aaron, give his majesty my hand :
    Tell him it was a hand that warded him
    From thousand dangers ; bid him bury it ;
    More hath it merited ; that let it have.
    As for my sons, say I account of them
    As jewels purchas'd at an easy price,
    And yet dear too, because I bought mine own.   200

Aar. I go, Andronicus : and for thy hand
    Look by and by to have thy sons with thee.
    (*aside*) Their heads, I mean. O, how this villany
    Doth fat me with the very thoughts of it !
    Let fools do good, and fair men call for grace,
    Aaron will have his soul black like his face.   *Exit*

Tit. O, here I lift this one hand up to heaven,

And bow this feeble ruin to the earth:
If any power pities wretched tears,
To that I call! *(to Lav.)* What, would thou kneel
    with me? 210
Do, then, dear heart; for heaven shall hear our prayers;
Or with our sighs we'll breathe the welkin dim,
And stain the sun with fog, as sometime clouds
When they do hug him in their melting bosoms.

Mar. O brother, speak with possibility,
And do not break into these deep extremes.

Tit. Is not my sorrow deep, having no bottom?
Then be my passions bottomless with them.

Mar. But yet let reason govern thy lament.

Tit. If there were reason for these miseries, 220
Then into limits could I bind my woes:
When heaven doth weep, doth not the earth o'erflow?
If the winds rage, doth not the sea wax mad,
Threatening the welkin with his big-swoln face?
And wilt thou have a reason for this coil?
I am the sea; hark, how her sighs do flow!
She is the weeping welkin, I the earth:
Then must my sea be moved with her sighs;
Then must my earth with her continual tears
Become a deluge, overflow'd and drown'd: 230
For why, my bowels cannot hide her woes,

But like a drunkard must I vomit them.

Then give me leave ; for losers will have leave

To ease their stomachs with their bitter tongues.

Enter a Messenger, with two heads and a hand

Mes. Worthy Andronicus, ill art thou repaid

For that good hand thou sent'st the emperor.

Here are the heads of thy two noble sons ;

And here 's thy hand, in scorn to thee sent back :

Thy griefs their sports : thy resolution mock'd :

That woe is me to think upon thy woes,   240

More than remembrance of my father's death. *Exit*

Mar. Now let hot Ætna cool in Sicily,

And be my heart an ever-burning hell !

These miseries are more than may be borne.

To weep with them that weep doth ease some deal,

But sorrow flouted at is double death.

Luc. Ah, that this sight should make so deep a wound,

And yet detested life not shrink thereat !

That ever death should let life bear his name,

Where life hath no more interest but to breathe !   250

Lavinia kisses Titus

Mar. Alas, poor heart, that kiss is comfortless

As frozen water to a starved snake.

Tit. When will this fearful slumber have an end ?

Mar. Now, farewell, flattery : die, Andronicus ;

Thou dost not slumber : see, thy two sons' heads,
Thy warlike hand, thy mangled daughter here,
Thy other banish'd son with this dear sight
Struck pale and bloodless, and thy brother, I,
Even like a stony image, cold and numb.
Ah, now no more will I control my griefs :   260
Rend off thy silver hair, thy other hand
Gnawing with thy teeth, and be this dismal sight
The closing up of our most wretched eyes :
Now is a time to storm, why art thou still ?

Tit. Ha, ha, ha !

Mar. Why dost thou laugh ? it fits not with this hour.

Tit. Why, I have not another tear to shed :
Besides, this sorrow is an enemy,
And would usurp upon my watery eyes,
And make them blind with tributary tears :   270
Then which way shall I find Revenge's cave ?
For these two heads do seem to speak to me,
And threat me I shall never come to bliss,
Till all these mischiefs be return'd again,
Even in their throats that have committed them.
Come, let me see what task I have to do,
You heavy people, circle me about,
That I may turn me to each one of you,
And swear unto my soul to right your wrongs.

The vow is made.   Come, brother, take a head ;   280
And in this hand the other will I bear.
And, Lavinia, thou shalt be employ'd in this ;   †
Bear thou my hand, sweet wench, between thy arms.
As for thee, boy, go get thee from my sight ;
Thou art an exile, and thou must not stay :
Hie to the Goths, and raise an army there,
And, if you love me, as I think you do,
Let's kiss and part, for we have much to do.

Exeunt all but Lucius

Luc. Farewell, Andronicus, my noble father,
The woful'st man that ever liv'd in Rome :   290
Farewell, proud Rome till Lucius come again,
He leaves his pledges dearer than his life :   †
Farewell, Lavinia, my noble sister ;
O, would thou wert as thou tofore hast been,
But now nor Lucius nor Lavinia lives
But in oblivion and hateful griefs.
If Lucius live, he will requite your wrongs ;
And make proud Saturnine and his empress
Beg at the gates, like Tarquin and his queen.
Now will I to the Goths and raise a power,   300
To be revenged on Rome and Saturnine.   *Exit*

{   SCENE II

A room in Titus's house.   A banquet set out

Enter Titus, Marcus, Lavinia, and young Lucius, a Boy

Tit. So, so ; now sit : and look you eat no more
Than will preserve just so much strength in us
As will revenge these bitter woes of ours.
Marcus, unknit that sorrow-wreathen knot :
Thy niece and I, poor creatures, want our hands,
And cannot passionate our tenfold grief
With folded arms.   This poor right hand of mine
Is left to tyrannize upon my breast ;
Who, when my heart, all mad with misery,
Beats in this hollow prison of my flesh,   10
Then thus I thump it down.
    (*to Lavinia*) Thou map of woe, that thus dost talk
      in signs,
When thy poor heart beats with outrageous beating
Thou canst not strike it thus to make it still.
Wound it with sighing, girl, kill it with groans ;
Or get some little knife between thy teeth,
And just against thy heart make thou a hole ;
That all the tears that thy poor eyes let fall
May run into that sink, and soaking in
Drown the lamenting fool in sea-salt tears.   20

*Mar.*Fie, brother, fie! teach her not thus to lay
    Such violent hands upon her tender life.

Tit. How now? has sorrow made thee dote already?
    Why, Marcus, no man should be mad but I.
    What violent hands can she lay on her life?
    Ah, wherefore dost thou urge the name of hands,
    To bid Æneas tell the tale twice o'er,   †
    How Troy was burnt and he made miserable?
    O, handle not the theme, to talk of hands,
    Lest we remember still that we have none.   30
    Fie, fie, how franticly I square my talk,
    As if we should forget we had no hands,
    If Marcus did not name the word of hands!
    Come, let's fall to; and, gentle girl, eat this:
    Here is no drink.   Hark, Marcus, what she says;
    I can interpret all her martyr'd signs;
    She says she drinks no other drink but tears,
    Brew'd with her sorrow, mesh'd upon her cheeks:
    Speechless complainer, I will learn thy thought;
    In thy dumb action will I be as perfect   40
    As begging hermits in their holy prayers:
    Thou shalt not sigh, nor hold thy stumps to heaven,
    Nor wink, nor nod, nor kneel, nor make a sign,
    But I of these will wrest an alphabet,
    And by still practice learn to know thy meaning.

Boy. Good grandsire, leave these bitter deep laments :
    Make my aunt merry with some pleasing tale.

Mar. Alas, the tender boy, in passion mov'd,
    Doth weep to see his grandsire's heaviness.

Tit. Peace, tender sapling ; thou art made of tears,   50
    And tears will quickly melt thy life away.

               Marcus strikes the dish with a knife

    What dost thou strike at, Marcus, with thy knife ?

Mar. At that that I have kill'd, my lord,—a fly.

Tit. Out on thee, murderer ! thou kill'st my heart ;
    Mine eyes are cloy'd with view of tyranny :
    A deed of death done on the innocent
    Becomes not Titus' brother : get thee gone ;
    I see thou art not for my company.

Mar. Alas, my lord, I have but kill'd a fly.

Tit. 'But?' How, if that fly had a father and mother?   60
    How would he hang his slender gilded wings,
    And buzz lamenting doings in the air,
    Poor harmless fly,
    That, with his pretty buzzing melody,
    Came here to make us merry, and thou hast kill'd him.

Mar. Pardon me, sir ; it was a black ill-favour'd fly,
    Like to the empress' Moor ; therefore I kill'd him.

Tit. O, O, O,
    Then pardon me for reprehending thee,

For thou hast done a charitable deed.   70
Give me thy knife, I will insult on him;
Flattering myself, as if it were the Moor
Come hither purposely to poison me.
There 's for thyself, and that 's for Tamora.
Ah, sirrah!
Yet, I think, we are not brought so low,
But that between us we can kill a fly
That comes in likeness of a coal-black Moor.

Mar. Alas, poor man! grief has so wrought on him,
He takes false shadows for true substances.   80

Tit. Come, take away.   Lavinia, go with me:
I 'll to thy closet; and go read with thee
Sad stories, chanced in the times of old.
Come, boy, and go with me: thy sight is young,
And thou shalt read when mine begin to dazzle.

                         Exeunt}

Act Fourth

SCENE I

Rome. *Titus's garden*

Enter young Lucius and Lavinia running after him, and the boy flies from her, with his books under his arm. Then enter Titus and Marcus

Boy. Help, grandsire, help ! my aunt Lavinia
    Follows me every where, I know not why :
    Good uncle Marcus, see how swift she comes.
    Alas, sweet aunt, I know not what you mean.
Mar. Stand by me, Lucius, do not fear thine aunt.
Tit. She loves thee, boy, too well to do thee harm.
Boy. Ay, when my father was in Rome she did.
Mar. What means my niece Lavinia by these signs ?
Tit. Fear her not, Lucius : somewhat doth she mean :
    See, Lucius, see how much she makes of thee :   10
    Somewhither would she have thee go with her.
    Ah, boy, Cornelia never with more care
    Read to her sons than she hath read to thee
    Sweet poetry and Tully's Orator.
Mar. Canst thou not guess wherefore she plies thee thus ?
Boy. My lord, I know not, I, nor can I guess,

Unless some fit or frenzy do possess her :
For I have heard my grandsire say full oft,
Extremity of griefs would make men mad ;
And I have read that Hecuba of Troy   20
Ran mad for sorrow : that made me to fear,
Although, my lord, I know my noble aunt
Loves me as dear as e'er my mother did,
And would not, but in fury, fright my youth,
Which made me down to throw my books and fly,
Causeless perhaps, but pardon me, sweet aunt,
And, madam, if my uncle Marcus go,
I will most willingly attend your ladyship.

Mar. Lucius, I will.

> *Lavinia turns over with her stumps the books*
> *which Lucius has let fall*

Tit. How now, Lavinia ?   Marcus, what means this ?   30
Some book there is that she desires to see.
Which is it, girl, of these ?   Open them, boy.
But thou art deeper read, and better skill'd :
Come, and take choice of all my library,
And so beguile thy sorrow, till the heavens
Reveal the damn'd contriver of this deed.
Why lifts she up her arms in sequence thus ?

Mar. I think she means that there were more than one
Confederate in the fact ; ay, more there was ;

Or else to heaven she heaves them for revenge. 40

Tit. Lucius, what book is that she tosseth so ?

Boy. Grandsire, 'tis Ovid's Metamorphoses :
My mother gave it me.

Mar. For love of her that 's gone,
Perhaps she cull'd it from among the rest.

Tit. Soft ! so busily she turns the leaves !
Help her :
What would she find ?   Lavinia, shall I read ?
This is the tragic tale of Philomel,
And treats of Tereus' treason and his rape ;
And rape, I fear, was root of thine annoy. 50

Mar. See, brother, see ; note how she quotes the leaves.

Tit. Lavinia, wert thou thus surpris'd, sweet girl,
Ravish'd and wrong'd, as Philomela was,
Forc'd in the ruthless, vast, and gloomy woods ?
See, see !
Ay, such a place there is, where we did hunt,—
O, had we never, never hunted there !—
Pattern'd by that the poet here describes,
By nature made for murders and for rapes.

Mar. O, why should nature build so foul a den, 60
Unless the gods delight in tragedies ?

Tit. Give signs, sweet girl, for here are none but friends,
What Roman lord it was durst do the deed :

Or slunk not Saturnine, as Tarquin erst,
That left the camp to sin in Lucrece' bed ?

Mar. Sit down, sweet niece : brother, sit down by me.
Apollo, Pallas, Jove, or Mercury,
Inspire me, that I may this treason find !
My lord, look here : look here, Lavinia :
This sandy plot is plain ; guide, if thou canst,   70
This after me.   (*He writes his name with his staff, and
      guides it with feet and mouth.*)   I have writ my
      name
Without the help of any hand at all.
Curs'd be that heart that forc'd us to this shift !
Write thou, good niece ; and here display at last
What God will have discover'd for revenge :
Heaven guide thy pen to print thy sorrows plain,
That we may know the traitors and the truth !

> *She takes the staff in her mouth, and guides it
> with her stumps, and writes*

Tit. O, do ye read, my lord, what she hath writ ?
  Stuprum.   Chiron.   Demetrius.

Mar. What, what, the lustful sons of Tamora,   80
Performers of this heinous, bloody deed ?

Tit. *Magni Dominator poli,*   †
  Tam lentus audis scelera, tam lentus vides ?

Mar. O, calm thee, gentle lord ; although I know

There is enough written upon this earth
To stir a mutiny in the mildest thoughts,
And arm the minds of infants to exclaims,
My lord, kneel down with me, Lavinia, kneel,
And kneel, sweet boy, the Roman Hector's hope ;
And swear with me, as, with the woful fere   90
And father of that chaste dishonoured dame,
Lord Junius Brutus sware for Lucrece' rape,
That we will prosecute by good advice
Mortal revenge upon these traitorous Goths,
And see their blood, or die with this reproach.

Tit. 'Tis sure enough, an you knew how.
But if you hunt these bear-whelps, then beware :
The dam will wake, and if she wind you once,
She 's with the lion deeply still in league,
And lulls him whilst she playeth on her back,   100
And when he sleeps will she do what she list.
You are a young huntsman, Marcus ; let alone ;
And, come, I will go get a leaf of brass,
And with a gad of steel will write these words,
And lay it by : the angry northern wind
Will blow these sands, like Sibyl's leaves, abroad,   †
And where 's your lesson then ?   Boy, what say you ?

Boy. I say, my lord, that if I were a man,
Their mother's bed-chamber should not be safe

  For these bad bondmen to the yoke of Rome.   110

Mar. Ay, that's my boy! thy father hath full oft

  For his ungrateful country done the like.

Boy. And, uncle, so will I, an if I live.

Tit. Come, go with me into mine armoury;

  Lucius, I'll fit thee, and withal my boy

  Shall carry from me to the empress' sons

  Presents that I intend to send them both:

  Come, come; thou'lt do thy message, wilt thou not?

Boy. Ay, with my dagger in their bosoms, grandsire.

Tit. No, boy, not so; I'll teach thee another course.   120

  Lavinia, come, Marcus, look to my house;

  Lucius and I'll go brave it at the court;

  Ay, marry, will we, sir; and we'll be waited on.

     Exeunt Titus, Lavinia, and young Lucius

Mar. O heavens, can you hear a good man groan,

  And not relent, or not compassion him?

  Marcus, attend him in his ecstasy,

  That hath more scars of sorrow in his heart

  Than foemen's marks upon his batter'd shield,

  But yet so just that he will not revenge.

  Revenge the heavens for old Andronicus!   *Exit* 130

SCENE II

The same.   A room in the palace

*Enter Aaron, Chiron, and Demetrius at one door ; and at
    another door, young Lucius, and an Attendant, with a
    bundle of weapons, and verses writ upon them*

Chi. Demetrius, here 's the son of Lucius ;
    He hath some message to deliver us.

Aar. Ay, some mad message from his mad grandfather.

Boy. My lords, with all the humbleness I may,
    I greet your honours from Andronicus.
    (*aside*) And pray the Roman gods confound you both !

Dem. Gramercy, lovely Lucius : what 's the news ?

Boy. (*aside*) [That you are both decipher'd, that 's the
            news,]
    For villains mark'd with rape.—May it please you,
    My grandsire, well advis'd, hath sent by me   10
    The goodliest weapons of his armoury
    To gratify your honourable youth,
    The hope of Rome ; for so he bid me say ;
    And so I do, and with his gifts present
    Your lordships, that, whenever you have need,
    You may be armed and appointed well :
    And so I leave you both, (*aside*) like bloody
            villains.   *Exeunt Boy and Attendant*

*Dem.*What's here ?   A scroll, and written round about ?
  Let's see :
  (*reads*) *Integer vitæ, scelerisque purus,*   † 20
     Non eget Mauri jaculis, nec arcu.
*Chi.*O, 'tis a verse in Horace ; I know it well :
  I read it in the grammar long ago.
*Aar.*Ay, just 'a verse in Horace ;' right, you have it.
  (*aside*) Now, what a thing it is to be an ass !
  Here's no sound jest : the old man hath found their
    guilt,
  And sends them weapons wrapp'd about with lines,
  That wound (beyond their feeling) to the quick.
  But were our witty empress well afoot,
  She would applaud Andronicus' conceit :   30
  But let her rest in her unrest awhile.—
  And now, young lords, was 't not a happy star
  Led us to Rome, strangers, and more than so,
  Captives, to be advanced to this height ?
  It did me good, before the palace gate
  To brave the tribune in his brother's hearing.
*Dem.*But me more good, to see so great a lord
  Basely insinuate, and send us gifts.
*Aar.*Had he not reason, Lord Demetrius ?
  Did you not use his daughter very friendly ?   40
*Dem.*I would we had a thousand Roman dames

    At such a bay, by turn to serve our lust.

Chi. A charitable wish and full of love.

Aar. Here lacks but your mother for to say amen.

Chi. And that would she for twenty thousand more.

Dem. Come, let us go, and pray to all the gods
    For our beloved mother in her pains.

Aar. (*aside*) Pray to the devils ; the gods have given us
       over.   *Trumpets sound within*

Dem. Why do the emperor's trumpets flourish thus ?

Chi. Belike, for joy the emperor hath a son.   50

Dem. Soft ! who comes here ?

                Enter Nurse

Nur.   Good morrow, lords :
    O, tell me, did you see Aaron the Moor ?

Aar. Well, more or less, or ne'er a whit at all,
    Here Aaron is ; and what with Aaron now ?

Nur. O gentle Aaron, we are all undone !
    Now help, or woe betide thee evermore !

Aar. Why, what a caterwauling dost thou keep !
    What dost thou wrap and fumble in thine arms ?

Nur. O, that which I would hide from heaven's eye,
    Our empress' shame, and stately Rome's disgrace !   60
    She is deliver'd, lords, she is deliver'd.

Aar. To whom ?

Nur.   I mean, she is brought a-bed.

*Aar.*Well, God give her good rest! What hath he
      sent her?

*Nur.*A devil.

Aar.   Why, then she is the devil's dam;
      A joyful issue.

*Nur.*A joyless, dismal, black and sorrowful issue:
                    Shows the Child, a blackamoor

      Here is the babe, as loathsome as a toad
      Amongst the fairest breeders of our clime:
      The empress sends it thee, thy stamp, thy seal,
      And bids thee christen it with thy dagger's point.   70

Aar.'Zounds, ye whore! is black so base a hue?
      Sweet blowse, you are a beauteous blossom, sure.

*Dem.*Villain, what hast thou done?

*Aar.*That which thou canst not undo.

Chi. Thou hast undone our mother.

[*Aar.*Villain, I have done thy mother.]

*Dem.*And therein, hellish dog, thou hast undone her.
      Woe to her chance, and damn'd her loathed choice!
      Accurs'd the offspring of so foul a fiend!

Chi. It shall not live.   80

*Aar.*It shall not die.

*Nur.*Aaron, it must; the mother wills it so.

*Aar.*What, must it, nurse? then let no man but I
      Do execution on my flesh and blood.

Dem. I 'll broach the tadpole on my rapier's point :
    Nurse, give it me : my sword shall soon dispatch it.
Aar. Sooner this sword shall plough thy bowels up.

        Takes the Child from the Nurse, and draws

    Stay, murderous villains ! will you kill your brother ?
    Now, by the burning tapers of the sky,
    That shone so brightly when this boy was got,   90
    He dies upon my scimitar's sharp point
    That touches this my first-born son and heir !
    I tell you, younglings, not Enceladus,   †
    With all his threatening band of Typhon's brood,
    Nor great Alcides, nor the god of war,
    Shall seize this prey out of his father's hands.
    What, what, ye sanguine, shallow-hearted boys !
    Ye white-limb'd walls ! ye alehouse painted signs !   †
    Coal-black is better than another hue,
    In that it scorns to bear another hue ;   100
    For all the water in the ocean
    Can never turn the swan's black legs to white,
    Although she lave them hourly in the flood.
    Tell the empress from me, I am of age
    To keep mine own, excuse it how she can.
Dem. Wilt thou betray thy noble mistress thus ?
Aar. My mistress is my mistress, this myself,
    The vigour and the picture of my youth :

This before all the world do I prefer ;
This maugre all the world will I keep safe,   110
Or some of you shall smoke for it in Rome.

Dem. By this our mother is for ever sham'd.

Chi. Rome will despise her for this foul escape.

Nur. The emperor in his rage will doom her death.

Chi. I blush to think upon this ignomy.

Aar. Why, there 's the privilege your beauty bears :
Fie, treacherous hue, that will betray with blushing
The close enacts and counsels of the heart !
Here 's a young lad fram'd of another leer :
Look, how the black slave smiles upon the father,   120
As who should say ' Old lad, I am thine own.'
He is your brother, lords, sensibly fed
Of that self-blood that first gave life to you ;
And from that womb where you imprisoned were
He is enfranchised and come to light :
Nay, he is your brother by the surer side,
Although my seal be stamped in his face.

Nur. Aaron, what shall I say unto the empress ?

Dem. Advise thee, Aaron, what is to be done,
And we will all subscribe to thy advice :   130
Save thou the child, so we may all be safe.

Aar. Then sit we down, and let us all consult.
My son and I will have the wind of you :

75

Keep there : now talk at pleasure of your safety.

They sit

Dem. How many women saw this child of his ?

Aar. Why, so, brave lords ! when we join in league,
 I am a lamb : but if you brave the Moor,
 The chafed boar, the mountain lioness,
 The ocean swells not so as Aaron storms.
 But say, again, how many saw the child ?   140

Nur. Cornelia the midwife and myself ;
 And no one else but the delivered empress.

Aar. The empress, the midwife, and yourself :
 Two may keep counsel when the third's away :
 Go to the empress, tell her this I said.

He kills the Nurse

 Week, week !
 So cries a pig prepared to the spit.

Dem. What mean'st thou, Aaron ? wherefore didst thou
  this ?

Aar. O Lord, sir, 'tis a deed of policy :
 Shall she live to betray this guilt of ours,   150
 A long-tongu'd babbling gossip ? no, lords, no :
 And now be it known to you my full intent.
 Not far, one Muliteus, my countryman,
 His wife but yesternight was brought to bed ;
 His child is like to her, fair as you are :

Go pack with him, and give the mother gold,
And tell them both the circumstance of all ;
And how by this their child shall be advanc'd,
And be received for the emperor's heir,
And substituted in the place of mine,   160
To calm this tempest whirling in the court ;
And let the emperor dandle him for his own.
Hark ye, lords ; you see I have given her physic,
                              Pointing to the Nurse

And you must needs bestow her funeral ;
The fields are near, and you are gallant grooms :
This done, see that you take no longer days,
But send the midwife presently to me.
The midwife and the nurse well made away,
Then let the ladies tattle what they please.

Chi. Aaron, I see thou wilt not trust the air   170
   With secrets.

Dem.   For this care of Tamora,
   Herself and hers are highly bound to thee.
      Exeunt Dem. and Chi. bearing off the Nurse's body

Aar. Now to the Goths, as swift as swallow flies ;
   There to dispose this treasure in mine arms,
   And secretly to greet the empress' friends.
   Come on, you thick-lipp'd slave, I'll bear you hence ;
   For it is you that puts us to our shifts :

77

I 'll make you feed on berries and on roots,
And feed on curds and whey, and suck the goat,
And cabin in a cave, and bring you up   180
To be a warrior and command a camp.   *Exit*

SCENE III

The same.   A public place

*Enter Titus, bearing arrows with letters at the ends of them ;
with him, Marcus, young Lucius, and other Gentlemen
(Publius, Sempronius, and Caius), with bows*

Tit. Come, Marcus, come ; kinsmen, this is the way.
Sir boy, let me see your archery ;
Look ye draw home enough, and 'tis there straight.
Terras Astræa reliquit :   †
Be you remember'd, Marcus, she 's gone, she 's fled.
Sirs, take you to your tools.   You, cousins, shall
Go sound the ocean, and cast your nets ;
Happily you may catch her in the sea ;
Yet there 's as little justice as at land :
No ; Publius and Sempronius, you must do it ;   10
'Tis you must dig with mattock and with spade,
And pierce the inmost centre of the earth :
Then, when you come to Pluto's region,

I pray you, deliver him this petition ;
Tell him, it is for justice and for aid,
And then it comes from old Andronicus,
Shaken with sorrows in ungrateful Rome.
Ah, Rome !   Well, well ; I made thee miserable
What time I threw the people's suffrages
On him that thus doth tyrannise o'er me.   20
Go get you gone ; and pray be careful all,
And leave you not a man-of-war unsearch'd :
This wicked emperor may have shipp'd her hence ;
And, kinsmen, then we may go pipe for justice.

*Mar.*O Publius, is not this a heavy case,
To see thy noble uncle thus distract ?

Pub. Therefore, my lord, it highly us concerns
By day and night to attend him carefully,
And feed his humour kindly as we may,
Till time beget some careful remedy.   30

*Mar.*Kinsmen, his sorrows are past remedy.
Join with the Goths, and with revengeful war
Take wreak on Rome for this ingratitude,
And vengeance on the traitor Saturnine.

Tit. Publius, how now ? how now, my masters ?
What, have you met with her ?

Pub. No, my good lord ; but Pluto sends you word,
If you will have Revenge from hell, you shall :

Marry, for Justice, she is so employ'd,
He thinks, with Jove in heaven, or somewhere else, 40
So that perforce you must needs stay a time.

Tit. He doth me wrong to feed me with delays.
I'll dive into the burning lake below,
And pull her out of Acheron by the heels.
Marcus, we are but shrubs, no cedars we,
No big-bon'd men fram'd of the Cyclops' size ;
But metal, Marcus, steel to the very back,
Yet wrung with wrongs more than our backs can
        bear :
And sith there's no justice in earth nor hell,
We will solicit heaven, and move the gods   50
To send down Justice for to wreak our wrongs.
Come, to this gear.   You are a good archer,
        Marcus ;   *He gives them the arrows*
Ad Jovem, that's for you : here, *Ad Apollinem* :
Ad Martem, that's for myself :
Here, boy, to Pallas : here, to Mercury :
To Saturn, Caius, not to Saturnine ;
You were as good to shoot against the wind.
To it, boy !   Marcus, loose when I bid.
Of my word, I have written to effect ;
There's not a god left unsolicited.   60

Mar. Kinsmen, shoot all your shafts into the court :

We will afflict the emperor in his pride.

Tit. Now, masters, draw.   (*They shoot.*)   O, well said, Lucius !
    Good boy, in Virgo's lap ; give it Pallas.

*Mar.*My lord, I aim a mile beyond the moon ;
    Your letter is with Jupiter by this.

Tit. Ha, ha !
    Publius, Publius, what hast thou done ?
    See, see, thou hast shot off one of Taurus' horns.

*Mar.*This was the sport, my lord : when Publius shot,   70
    The Bull, being gall'd, gave Aries such a knock
    That down fell both the Ram's horns in the court ;
    And who should find them but the empress' villain ?
    She laugh'd, and told the Moor he should not choose
    But give them to his master for a present.

Tit. Why, there it goes : God give his lordship joy.
    Enter a Clown, with a basket, and two pigeons in it
    News, news from heaven ! Marcus, the post is come.
    Sirrah, what tidings ? have you any letters ?
    Shall I have justice ? what says Jupiter ?

Clo. Ho, the gibbet-maker ? he says that he hath taken   80
them down again, for the man must not be hang'd
till the next week.

Tit. But what says Jupiter, I ask thee ?

Clo. Alas, sir, I know not Jupiter ; I never drank with
him in all my life.

Tit. Why, villain, art not thou the carrier?

Clo. Ay, of my pigeons, sir; nothing else.

Tit. Why, didst thou not come from heaven?

Clo. From heaven? alas, sir, I never came there:
God forbid I should be so bold, to press to heaven   90
in my young days. Why, I am going with my
pigeons to the tribunal plebs, to take up a matter
of brawl betwixt my uncle and one of the emperial's
men.

Mar. Why, sir, that is as fit as can be to serve for your
oration; and let him deliver the pigeons to the
emperor from you.

Tit. Tell me, can you deliver an oration to the emperor
with a grace?

Clo. Nay, truly, sir, I could never say grace in all my life. 100

Tit. Sirrah, come hither: make no more ado,
But give your pigeons to the emperor:
By me thou shalt have justice at his hands.
Hold, hold; meanwhile here's money for thy charges.
Give me pen and ink.
Sirrah, can you with a grace deliver a supplication?

Clo. Ay, sir.

Tit. Then here is a supplication for you. And when you
come to him, at the first approach you must kneel,
then kiss his foot, then deliver up your pigeons, and 110

then look for your reward.   I'll be at hand, sir;
    see you do it bravely.

Clo. I warrant you, sir, let me alone.

Tit. Sirrah, hast thou a knife ? come, let me see it.
    Here, Marcus, fold it in the oration ;
    For thou hast made it like an humble suppliant :
    And when thou hast given it to the emperor,
    Knock at my door, and tell me what he says.

Clo. God be with you, sir ; I will.   *Exit*

Tit. Come, Marcus, let us go.   Publius, follow me.   120
                                      Exeunt

SCENE IV

The same.   Before the palace

Enter Saturninus, Tamora, Chiron, Demetrius, Lords, and
    others ; Saturninus with the Arrows in his hand that
    Titus shot

Sat. Why, lords, what wrongs are these ! was ever seen
    An emperor in Rome thus overborne,
    Troubled, confronted thus, and for the extent
    Of egal justice us'd in such contempt ?
    My lords, you know, as know the mightful gods,
    However these disturbers of our peace

Buzz in the people's ears, there nought hath pass'd
But even with law against the wilful sons
Of old Andronicus.   And what an if
His sorrows have so overwhelm'd his wits ?   10
Shall we be thus afflicted in his wreaks,
His fits, his frenzy and his bitterness ?
And now he writes to heaven for his redress :
See, here 's to Jove, and this to Mercury ;
This to Apollo ; this to the god of war :
Sweet scrolls to fly about the streets of Rome !
What 's this but libelling against the senate,
And blazoning our unjustice every where ?
A goodly humour, is it not, my lords ?
As who would say, in Rome no justice were.   20
But if I live, his feigned ecstasies
Shall be no shelter to these outrages :
But he and his shall know that justice lives
In Saturninus' health ; whom, if he sleep,
He 'll so awake, as he in fury shall
Cut off the proud'st conspirator that lives.

*Tam.*My gracious lord, my lovely Saturnine,
Lord of my life, commander of my thoughts,
Calm thee, and bear the faults of Titus' age,
The effects of sorrow for his valiant sons,   30
Whose loss hath pierced him deep and scarr'd his heart ;

And rather comfort his distressed plight
Than prosecute the meanest or the best
For these contempts. *(aside)* Why, thus it shall become
High-witted Tamora to gloze with all :
But, Titus, I have touch'd thee to the quick,
Thy life-blood out : if Aaron now be wise,
Then is all safe, the anchor in the port.

Enter Clown

How now, good fellow ! wouldst thou speak with us ?

Clo. Yea, forsooth, an your mistership be emperial.   40

Tam. Empress I am, but yonder sits the emperor.

Clo. 'Tis he.   God and Saint Stephen give you godden :
I have brought you a letter and a couple of pigeons
here.   *Saturninus reads the letter*

Sat. Go, take him away, and hang him presently.

Clo. How much money must I have ?

Tam. Come, sirrah, you must be hang'd.

Clo. Hang'd ! by 'r lady, then I have brought up a neck
to a fair end.   *Exit, guarded*

Sat. Despiteful and intolerable wrongs !   50
Shall I endure this monstrous villany ?
I know from whence this same device proceeds ;
May this be borne ?   As if his traitorous sons,
That died by law for murder of our brother,
Have by my means been butcher'd wrongfully !

Go, drag the villain hither by the hair
Nor age nor honour shall shape privilege :
For this proud mock I 'll be thy slaughter-man ;
Sly frantic wretch, that holp'st to make me great,
In hope thyself should govern Rome and me.   60

Enter Æmilius

What news with thee, Æmilius ?

Æm. Arm, my lords ; Rome never had more cause.
The Goths have gather'd head, and with a power
Of high-resolved men, bent to the spoil,
They hither march amain, under conduct
Of Lucius, son to old Andronicus ;
Who threats, in course of this revenge, to do
As much as ever Coriolanus did.

Sat. Is warlike Lucius general of the Goths ?
These tidings nip me, and I hang the head   70
As flowers with frost, or grass beat down with storms :
Ay, now begin our sorrows to approach :
'Tis he the common people love so much
Myself hath often heard them say,
When I have walked like a private man,
That Lucius' banishment was wrongfully,
And they have wish'd that Lucius were their emperor.

Tam. Why should you fear ? is not your city strong ?

Sat. Ay, but the citizens favour Lucius,

       And will revolt from me to succour him.   80

*Tam.*King, be thy thoughts imperious, like thy name.

       Is the sun dimm'd, that gnats do fly in it?

       The eagle suffers little birds to sing,

       And is not careful what they mean thereby,

       Knowing that with the shadow of his wings

       He can at pleasure stint their melody:

       Even so mayst thou the giddy men of Rome.

       Then cheer thy spirit: for know, thou emperor,

       I will enchant the old Andronicus

       With words more sweet, and yet more dangerous,   90

       Than baits to fish, or honey-stalks to sheep;

       Whenas the one is wounded with the bait,

       The other rotted with delicious feed.

Sat. But he will not entreat his son for us.

*Tam.*If Tamora entreat him, then he will:

       For I can smooth, and fill his aged ears

       With golden promises; that, were his heart

       Almost impregnable, his old ears deaf,

       Yet should both ear and heart obey my tongue.

       (*to Æmilius*) Go thou before to be our ambassador: 100

       Say that the emperor requests a parley

       Of warlike Lucius, and appoint the meeting

       Even at his father's house, the old Andronicus.

Sat. Æmilius, do this message honourably:

And if he stand in hostage for his safety,
Bid him demand what pledge will please him best.

Æm. Your bidding shall I do effectually.　　　　*Exit*

Tam. Now will I to that old Andronicus,
And temper him with all the art I have,
To pluck proud Lucius from the warlike Goths.　　110
And now, sweet emperor, be blithe again,
And bury all thy fear in my devices.

Sat. Then go successantly, and plead to him.　　*Exeunt*

Act Fifth

SCENE I

Plains near Rome

Flourish.　Enter Lucius and Goths, with drum and colours

Luc. Approved warriors, and my faithful friends,
I have received letters from great Rome,
Which signify what hate they bear their emperor,
And how desirous of our sight they are.
Therefore, great lords, be, as your titles witness,
Imperious, and impatient of your wrongs ;
And wherein Rome hath done you any scath,

       Let him make treble satisfaction.

First Goth. Brave slip, sprung from the great Andronicus,
    Whose name was once our terror, now our comfort;   10
    Whose high exploits, and honourable deeds,
    Ingrateful Rome requites with foul contempt,
    Be bold in us; we'll follow where thou lead'st,
    Like stinging bees in hottest summer's day,
    Led by their master to the flowered fields,
    And be aveng'd on cursed Tamora.

All the Goths. And as he saith, so say we all with him.

Luc. I humbly thank him, and I thank you all.
    But who comes here, led by a lusty Goth?

    Enter a Goth, leading Aaron with his Child in his arms

Sec. Goth. Renowned Lucius, from our troops I stray'd   20
    To gaze upon a ruinous monastery;
    And, as I earnestly did fix mine eye
    Upon the wasted building, suddenly
    I heard a child cry underneath a wall.
    I made unto the noise; when soon I heard
    The crying babe controll'd with this discourse:
    'Peace, tawny slave, half me and half thy dam!
    Did not thy hue bewray whose brat thou art,
    Had nature lent thee but thy mother's look,
    Villain, thou mightst have been an emperor: 30
    But where the bull and cow are both milk-white,

They never do beget a coal-black calf.
Peace, villain, peace!'—even thus he rates the babe—
'For I must bear thee to a trusty Goth;
Who, when he knows thou art the empress' babe,
Will hold thee dearly for thy mother's sake.'
With this, my weapon drawn, I rush'd upon him,
Surpris'd him suddenly, and brought him hither,
To use as you think needful of the man.

Luc. O worthy Goth, this is the incarnate devil   40
That robb'd Andronicus of his good hand;
This is the pearl that pleas'd your empress' eye;   †·
And here's the base fruit of her burning lust.
Say, wall-ey'd slave, whither wouldst thou convey
This growing image of thy fiend-like face?
Why dost not speak? what, deaf? not a word?
A halter, soldiers! hang him on this tree,
And by his side his fruit of bastardy.

Aar. Touch not the boy; he is of royal blood.

Luc. Too like the sire for ever being good.   50
First hang the child, that he may see it sprawl;
A sight to vex the father's soul withal.
Get me a ladder.

          A ladder brought, which Aaron is made to ascend

Aar.   Lucius, save the child,
And bear it from me to the emperess.

If thou do this, I'll show thee wondrous things,
That highly may advantage thee to hear;
If thou wilt not, befal what may befal,
I'll speak no more, but Vengeance rot you all.

Luc. Say on: an if it please me which thou speak'st,
Thy child shall live, and I will see it nourish'd.   60

Aar. An if it please thee? why, assure thee, Lucius,
'Twill vex thy soul to hear what I shall speak;
For I must talk of murders, rapes and massacres,
Acts of black night, abominable deeds,
Complots of mischief, treason, villanies
Ruthful to hear, yet piteously perform'd:
And this shall all be buried in my death,
Unless thou swear to me my child shall live.

Luc. Tell on thy mind; I say thy child shall live.

Aar. Swear that he shall, and then I will begin.   70

Luc. Who should I swear by? thou believ'st no god:
That granted, how canst thou believe an oath?

Aar. What if I do not? as, indeed, I do not;
Yet, for I know thou art religious,
And hast a thing within thee called conscience,
With twenty popish tricks and ceremonies,
Which I have seen thee careful to observe,
Therefore I urge thy oath; for that I know
An idiot holds his bauble for a god,

And keeps the oath which by that god he swears, 80
To that I 'll urge him : therefore thou shalt vow
By that same god, what god soe'er it be,
That thou adorest and hast in reverence,
To save my boy, to nourish and bring him up ;
Or else I will discover nought to thee.

Luc. Even by my god I sware to thee I will.

Aar. First know thou, I begot him on the empress.

Luc. O most insatiate, and luxurious woman !

Aar. Tut, Lucius, this was but a deed of charity
To that which thou shalt hear of me anon. 90
'Twas her two sons that murder'd Bassianus :
They cut thy sister's tongue, and ravish'd her,
And cut her hands, and trimm'd her as thou saw'st.

Luc. O detestable villain ! call'st thou that trimming ?

Aar. Why, she was wash'd and cut and trimm'd, and 'twas
Trim sport for them that had the doing of it.

Luc. O barbarous, beastly villains, like thyself !

Aar. Indeed, I was their tutor to instruct them :
That codding spirit had they from their mother,
As sure a card as ever won the set ; 100
That bloody mind, I think, they learn'd of me,
As true a dog as ever fought at head.
Well, let my deeds be witness of my worth.
I train'd thy brethren to that guileful hole,

Where the dead corpse of Bassianus lay:
I wrote the letter that thy father found,
And hid the gold within the letter mention'd,
Confederate with the queen and her two sons:
And what not done, that thou hast cause to rue,
Wherein I had no stroke of mischief in it?   110
I play'd the cheater for thy father's hand;
And, when I had it, drew myself apart,
And almost broke my heart with extreme laughter:
I pried me through the crevice of a wall
When for his hand he had his two sons' heads;
Beheld his tears and laugh'd so heartily,
That both mine eyes were rainy like to his:
And when I told the empress of this sport,
She swounded almost at my pleasing tale,
And for my tidings gave me twenty kisses.   120

First Goth. What, canst thou say all this, and never blush?
Aar. Ay, like a black dog, as the saying is.
Luc. Art thou not sorry for these heinous deeds?
Aar. Ay, that I had not done a thousand more.
Even now I curse the day—and yet, I think,
Few come within the compass of my curse—
Wherein I did not some notorious ill:
As kill a man, or else devise his death;
Ravish a maid, or plot the way to do it:

Accuse some innocent, and forswear myself ;   130
Set deadly enmity between two friends ;
Make poor men's cattle break their necks ;
Set fire on barns and hay-stacks in the night,
And bid the owners quench them with their tears.
Oft have I digg'd up dead men from their graves,
And set them upright at their dear friends' door,
Even when their sorrows almost was forgot ;
And on their skins, as on the bark of trees,
Have with my knife carv'd in Roman letters
' Let not your sorrow die, though I am dead.'   140
Tut, I have done a thousand dreadful things
As willingly as one would kill a fly ;
And nothing grieves me heartily indeed,
But that I cannot do ten thousand more.

Luc. Bring down the devil ; for he must not die
So sweet a death as hanging presently.

Aar. If there be devils, would I were a devil,
To live and burn in everlasting fire,
So I might have your company in hell,
But to torment you with my bitter tongue !   150

Luc. Sirs, stop his mouth, and let him speak no more.

Enter a Goth

Third Goth. My lord, there is a messenger from Rome
Desires to be admitted to your presence.

Luc. Let him come near.

Enter Æmilius

Welcome, Æmilius: what's the news from Rome?

Æm. Lord Lucius, and you princes of the Goths,
The Roman emperor greets you all by me;
And, for he understands you are in arms,
He craves a parley at your father's house,
Willing you to demand your hostages,   16c
And they shall be immediately deliver'd.

First Goth. What says our general?

Luc. Æmilius, let the emperor give his pledges
Unto my father, and my uncle Marcus,
And we will come.   March away.

Flourish.   Exeunt

SCENES II, III

Rome.   Before Titus's house

Enter Tamora, Demetrius, and Chiron, disguised

Tam. Thus, in this strange and sad habiliment,
I will encounter with Andronicus,
And say I am Revenge, sent from below
To join with him and right his heinous wrongs.
Knock at his study, where, they say, he keeps,

95

        To ruminate strange plots of dire revenge ;
        Tell him Revenge is come to join with him,
        And work confusion on his enemies.

      They knock, and Titus opens his study door

Tit. Who doth molest my contemplation ?

      Is it your trick to make me ope the door,   10

      That so my sad decrees may fly away,

      And all my study be to no effect ?

      You are deceiv'd : for what I mean to do

      See here in bloody lines I have set down ;

      And what is written shall be executed.

Tam. Titus, I am come to talk with thee.

Tit. No, not a word : how can I grace my talk,

      Wanting a hand to give it action ?

      Thou hast the odds of me ; therefore no more.

Tam. If thou didst know me, thou wouldst talk with me.   20

Tit. I am not mad ; I know thee well enough :

      Witness this wretched stump, witness these crimson
            lines ;

      Witness these trenches made by grief and care ;

      Witness the tiring day and heavy night ;

      Witness all sorrow, that I know thee well

      For our proud empress, mighty Tamora :

      Is not thy coming for my other hand ?

Tam. Know, thou sad man, I am not Tamora ;

She is thy enemy, and I thy friend :

I am Revenge ; sent from the infernal kingdom,   30

To ease the gnawing vulture of thy mind,

By working wreakful vengeance on thy foes.

Come down and welcome me to this world's light ;

Confer with me of murder and of death :

There 's not a hollow cave or lurking-place,

No vast obscurity or misty vale,

Where bloody murder or detested rape

Can couch for fear, but I will find them out,

And in their ears tell them my dreadful name,

Revenge, which makes the foul offender quake.   40

Tit. Art thou Revenge ? and art thou sent to me,

To be a torment to mine enemies ?

Tam. I am ; therefore come down and welcome me.

Tit. Do me some service ere I come to thee.

Lo, by thy side where Rape and Murder stands ;

Now give some surance that thou art Revenge,

Stab them, or tear them on thy chariot-wheels ;

And then I 'll come and be thy waggoner,

And whirl along with thee about the globes.

Provide thee two proper palfreys, black as jet,   50

To hale thy vengeful waggon swift away,

And find out murderers in their guilty caves :

And when thy car is loaden with their heads,

    I will dismount, and by the waggon-wheel
    Trot like a servile footman all day long,
    Even from Hyperion's rising in the east
    Until his very downfall in the sea :
    And day by day I 'll do this heavy task,
    So thou destroy Rapine and Murder there.

Tam. These are my ministers and come with me.   60

Tit. Are these thy ministers ? what are they call'd ?

Tam. Rape and Murder ; therefore called so,
    'Cause they take vengeance of such kind of men.

Tit. Good Lord, how like the empress' sons they are,
    And you the empress ! but we worldly men
    Have miserable, mad, mistaking eyes.
    O sweet Revenge, now do I come to thee ;
    And, if one arm's embracement will content thee,
    I will embrace thee in it by and by.   *Exit*

Tam. This closing with him fits his lunacy :   70
    Whate'er I forge to feed his brain-sick fits,
    Do you uphold and maintain in your speeches,
    For now he firmly takes me for Revenge ;
    And, being credulous in this mad thought,
    I 'll make him send for Lucius his son ;
    And, whilst I at a banquet hold him sure,
    I 'll find some cunning practice out of hand,
    To scatter and disperse the giddy Goths,

Or at the least make them his enemies.
See, here he comes, and I must ply my theme.   80

Enter Titus

Tit. Long have I been forlorn, and all for thee :
Welcome, dread Fury, to my woful house :
Rapine and Murder, you are welcome too :
How like the empress and her sons you are !
Well are you fitted, had you but a Moor :
Could not all hell afford you such a devil ?
For well I wot the empress never wags
But in her company there is a Moor ;
And, would you represent our queen aright,
It were convenient you had such a devil :   90
But welcome, as you are.   What shall we do ?

Tam. What wouldst thou have us do, Andronicus ?

Dem. Show me a murderer, I'll deal with him.

Chi. Show me a villain that hath done a rape,
And I am sent to be reveng'd on him.

Tam. Show me a thousand that have done thee wrong,
And I will be revenged on them all.

Tit. Look round about the wicked streets of Rome,
And when thou find'st a man that's like thyself,
Good Murder, stab him ; he's a murderer.   100
Go thou with him, and when it is thy hap
To find another that is like to thee,

Good Rapine, stab him; he's a ravisher.
Go thou with them; and in the emperor's court
There is a queen, attended by a Moor;
Well mayst thou know her by thine own proportion,
For up and down she doth resemble thee:
I pray thee, do on them some violent death;
They have been violent to me and mine.

Tam. Well hast thou lesson'd us; this shall we do.   110
But would it please thee, good Andronicus,
To send for Lucius, thy thrice valiant son,
Who leads towards Rome a band of warlike Goths,
And bid him come and banquet at thy house;
When he is here, even at thy solemn feast,
I will bring in the empress and her sons,
The emperor himself, and all thy foes;
And at thy mercy shall they stoop and kneel,
And on them shalt thou ease thy angry heart.
What says Andronicus to this device?   120

Tit. Marcus, my brother! 'tis sad Titus calls.

Enter Marcus

Go, gentle Marcus, to thy nephew Lucius;
Thou shalt inquire him out among the Goths:
Bid him repair to me and bring with him
Some of the chiefest princes of the Goths:
Bid him encamp his soldiers where they are:

Tell him the emperor and the empress too
Feast at my house, and he shall feast with them.
This do thou for my love, and so let him,
As he regards his aged father's life.   130

Mar. This will I do, and soon return again.   *Exit*

Tam. Now will I hence about thy business,
  And take my ministers along with me.

Tit. Nay, nay, let Rape and Murder stay with me ;
  Or else I 'll call my brother back again,
  And cleave to no revenge but Lucius.

Tam. (*aside to her sons*) What say you, boys ? will you
   bide with him,
  Whiles I go tell my lord the emperor
  How I have govern'd our determined jest ?
  Yield to his humour, smooth and speak him fair,   140
  And tarry with him till I turn again.

Tit. (*aside*) I know them all, though they suppose me
   mad ;
  And will o'er-reach them in their own devices :
  A pair of cursed hell-hounds and their dam.

Dem. Madam, depart at pleasure ; leave us here.

Tam. Farewell, Andronicus : Revenge now goes
  To lay a complot to betray thy foes.

Tit. I know thou dost ; and, sweet Revenge, farewell.
         Exit Tamora

Chi. Tell us, old man, how shall we be employ'd?

Tit. Tut, I have work enough for you to do.   150
Publius, come hither, Caius, and Valentine!

Enter Publius and others

Pub. What is your will?

Tit. Know you these two?

Pub. The empress' sons I take them, Chiron and
Demetrius.

Tit. Fie, Publius, fie! thou art too much deceiv'd;
The one is Murder, Rape is the other's name;
And therefore bind them, gentle Publius:
Caius and Valentine, lay hands on them:
Oft have you heard me wish for such an hour,   160
And now I find it; therefore bind them sure;
[And stop their mouths, if they begin to cry.]   *Exit
Publius, &c. lay hold on Chiron and Demetrius*

Chi. Villains, forbear! we are the empress' sons.

Pub. And therefore do we what we are commanded.
Stop close their mouths, let them not speak a word.
Is he sure bound? look that you bind them fast.

*Re-enter Titus, with Lavinia; he bearing a knife,
and she a basin*

Tit. Come, come, Lavinia; look, thy foes are bound.
Sirs, stop their mouths, let them not speak to me;
But let them hear what fearful words I utter.

O villains, Chiron and Demetrius !   170
Here stands the spring whom you have stain'd with
     mud,
This goodly summer with your winter mix'd.
You kill'd her husband, and for that vile fault
Two of her brothers were condemn'd to death,
My hand cut off and made a merry jest ;
Both her sweet hands, her tongue, and that more dear
Than hands or tongue, her spotless chastity,
Inhuman traitors, you constrain'd and forc'd.
What would you say, if I should let you speak ?
Villains, for shame you could not beg for grace.   180
Hark, wretches, how I mean to martyr you.
This one hand yet is left to cut your throats,
Whilst that Lavinia 'tween her stumps doth hold
The basin that receives your guilty blood.
You know your mother means to feast with me,
And calls herself Revenge, and thinks me mad :
Hark, villains !   I will grind your bones to dust,
And with your blood and it I'll make a paste ;
And of the paste a coffin I will rear,
And make two pasties of your shameful heads ;   190
And bid that strumpet, your unhallow'd dam,
Like to the earth, swallow her own increase.
This is the feast that I have bid her to,

And this the banquet she shall surfeit on ;
For worse than Philomel you us'd my daughter,
And worse than Progne I will be reveng'd :
And now prepare your throats.   Lavinia, come,
Receive the blood : and when that they are dead,
Let me go grind their bones to powder small,
And with this hateful liquor temper it ;   200
And in that paste let their vile heads be bak'd.
Come, come, be every one officious
To make this banquet ; which I wish may prove
More stern and bloody than the Centaurs' feast.

He cuts their throats

So, now bring them in, for I 'll play the cook,
And see them ready against their mother comes.

Exeunt, bearing the dead bodies

Enter Lucius, Marcus, and Goths, with Aaron, prisoner

Luc. Uncle Marcus, since it is my father's mind
   That I repair to Rome, I am content.
First Goth. And ours with thine, befall what fortune will.
Luc. Good uncle, take you in this barbarous Moor,

This ravenous tiger, this accursed devil ;
Let him receive no sustenance, fetter him,
Till he be brought unto the empress' face,
For testimony of her foul proceedings :
And see the ambush of our friends be strong ;
I fear the emperor means no good to us.   10

Aar. Some devil whisper curses in mine ear,
    And prompt me, that my tongue may utter forth
    The venomous malice of my swelling heart !

Luc. Away, inhuman dog ! unhallow'd slave !
    Sirs, help our uncle to convey him in,

        Exeunt Goths, with Aaron.   Flourish within

    The trumpets show the emperor is at hand.

        Enter Saturninus and Tamora, with Æmilius, Tribunes,
            Senators, and others

Sat. What, hath the firmament moe suns than one ?

Luc. What boots it thee to call thyself a sun ?

Mar. Rome's emperor, and nephew, break the parle ;
    These quarrels must be quietly debated.   20
    The feast is ready, which the careful Titus
    Hath ordain'd to an honourable end,
    For peace, for love, for league and good to Rome :
    Please you, therefore, draw nigh, and take your places.

Sat. Marcus, we will.

        Hautboys sound.   A table brought in

*Enter Titus, like a Cook, placing the meat on the table, and
Lavinia with a veil over her face, young Lucius, and others*

Tit. Welcome, my gracious lord ; welcome, dread queen ;
Welcome, ye warlike Goths ; welcome, Lucius ;
And welcome, all : although the cheer be poor,
'Twill fill your stomachs ; please you eat of it.

Sat. Why art thou thus attir'd, Andronicus ?   30

Tit. Because I would be sure to have all well,
To entertain your highness and your empress.

Tam. We are beholding to you, good Andronicus.

Tit. An if your highness knew my heart, you were.
My lord the emperor, resolve me this :
Was it well done of rash Virginius
To slay his daughter with his own right hand,
Because she was enforc'd, stain'd, and deflower'd ?

Sat. It was, Andronicus.

Tit. Your reason, mighty lord ?   40

Sat. Because the girl should not survive her shame,
And by her presence still renew his sorrows.

Tit. A reason mighty, strong and effectual,
A pattern, precedent, and lively warrant,
For me, most wretched, to perform the like.
Die, die, Lavinia, and thy shame with thee,
And with thy shame thy father's sorrow die !

Kills Lavinia

Sat. What hast thou done, unnatural and unkind?

Tit. Kill'd her for whom my tears have made me blind.
    I am as woful as Virginius was,   50
    And have a thousand times more cause than he
    [To do this outrage, and it now is done.]

Sat. What, was she ravish'd? tell who did the deed.

Tit. Will 't please you eat? will 't please your highness
    feed?

Tam. Why hast thou slain thine only daughter thus?

Tit. Not I; 'twas Chiron and Demetrius:
    They ravish'd her, and cut away her tongue;
    And they, 'twas they, that did her all this wrong.

Sat. Go fetch them hither to us presently.

Tit. Why, there they are both, baked in that pie;   60
    Whereof their mother daintily hath fed,
    Eating the flesh that she herself hath bred.
    'Tis true, 'tis true; witness my knife's sharp point.
                         Kills Tamora

Sat. Die, frantic wretch, for this accursed deed!
                             Kills Titus

Luc. Can the son's eye behold his father bleed?
    There 's meed for meed, death for a deadly deed!
        Kills Saturninus.   A great tumult.   Lucius,
          Marcus, and others go up into the balcony

Mar. You sad-fac'd men, people and sons of Rome,

By uproars sever'd, as a flight of fowl
Scatter'd by winds and high tempestuous gusts,
O, let me teach you how to knit again   70
This scatter'd corn into one mutual sheaf,
These broken limbs again into one body.

Roman Lord. Lest Rome herself be bane unto herself;   †
And she whom mighty kingdoms court'sy to,
Like a forlorn and desperate castaway,
Do shameful execution on herself,
But if my frosty signs and chaps of age,
Grave witnesses of true experience,
Cannot induce you to attend my words,
(*to Lucius*) Speak, Rome's dear friend: as erst our
      ancestor,   80
When with his solemn tongue he did discourse
To love-sick Dido's sad attending ear   †
The story of that baleful burning night,
When subtle Greeks surpris'd King Priam's Troy;
Tell us what Sinon hath bewitch'd our ears,
Or who hath brought the fatal engine in
That gives our Troy, our Rome, the civil wound.
My heart is not compact of flint nor steel,
Nor can I utter all our bitter grief,
But floods of tears will drown my oratory,   90
And break my utterance, even in the time

When it should move you to attend me most,
Lending your kind commiseration.
Here is a Captain, let him tell the tale ;
Your hearts will throb and weep to hear him speak.

Luc. Then, noble auditory, be it known to you,
That cursed Chiron and Demetrius
Were they that murder'd our emperor's brother,
And they it were that ravished our sister :
For their fell faults our brothers were beheaded,   100
Our father's tears despis'd, and basely cozen'd
Of that true hand that fought Rome's quarrel out,
And sent her enemies unto the grave.
Lastly, myself unkindly banished,
The gates shut on me, and turn'd weeping out,
To beg relief among Rome's enemies ;
Who drown'd their enmity in my true tears,
And op'd their arms to embrace me as a friend.
I am the turn'd forth, be it known to you,
That have preserv'd her welfare in my blood,   110
And from her bosom took the enemy's point,
Sheathing the steel in my adventurous body.
Alas, you know I am no vaunter, I ;
My scars can witness, dumb although they **are,**
That my report is just and full of truth.
But, soft ! methinks I do digress too much,

Citing my worthless praise : O, pardon me ;
For when no friends are by, men praise themselves.
Mar. Now is my turn to speak.   Behold the child :
> *Pointing to the Child in the arms of an Attendant*

Of this was Tamora delivered ;   120
The issue of an irreligious Moor,
Chief architect and plotter of these woes :
The villain is alive in Titus' house,
And as he is, to witness this is true.
Now judge what cause had Titus to revenge
These wrongs, unspeakable, past patience,
Or more than any living man could bear.
Now you have heard the truth, what say you, Romans ?
Have we done aught amiss, show us wherein,
And, from the place where you behold us now,   130
The poor remainder of Andronici
Will, hand in hand, all headlong cast us down,
And on the ragged stones beat forth our brains,
And make a mutual closure of our house.
Speak, Romans, speak, and if you say we shall,
Lo, hand in hand, Lucius and I will fall.
Æm. Come, come, thou reverend man of Rome,
And bring our emperor gently in thy hand,
Lucius our emperor ; for well I know
The common voice do cry it shall be so.   140

All. Lucius, all hail, Rome's royal emperor !

Mar. Go, go into old Titus' sorrowful house,

To Attendants

And hither hale that misbelieving Moor,

To be adjudg'd some direful slaughtering death,

As punishment for his most wicked life.

Exeunt Attendants

Lucius, Marcus, and the others descend

All. Lucius, all hail, Rome's gracious governor !

Luc. Thanks, gentle Romans : may I govern so,

To heal Rome's harms and wipe away her woe !

But, gentle people, give me aim awhile,

For nature puts me to a heavy task ;   150

Stand all aloof ; but, uncle, draw you near,

To shed obsequious tears upon this trunk.

O, take this warm kiss on thy pale cold lips,

Kissing Titus

These sorrowful drops upon thy blood-stain'd face,

The last true duties of thy noble son !

Mar. Tear for tear and loving kiss for kiss

Thy brother Marcus tenders on thy lips :

O, were the sum of these that I should pay

Countless and infinite, yet would I pay them !

Luc. Come hither, boy : come, come, and learn of us   160

To melt in showers : thy grandsire lov'd thee well,

Many a time he danc'd thee on his knee,
Sung thee asleep, his loving breast thy pillow ;
Many a matter hath he told to thee,
Meet and agreeing with thine infancy ;
In that respect then, like a loving child,
Shed yet some small drops from thy tender spring,
Because kind nature doth require it so :
Friends should associate friends in grief and woe :
Bid him farewell ; commit him to the grave ;   170
Do him that kindness, and take leave of him.

Boy. O grandsire, grandsire ! even with all my heart
Would I were dead, so you did live again !
O Lord, I cannot speak to him for weeping ;
My tears will choke me, if I ope my mouth.

Re-enter Attendants with Aaron

A Roman. You sad Andronici, have done with woes :
Give sentence on this execrable wretch,
That hath been breeder of these dire events.

Luc. Set him breast-deep in earth, and famish him ;
There let him stand and rave and cry for food :   180
If any one relieves or pities him,
For the offence he dies.   This is our doom :
Some stay to see him fasten'd in the earth.

Aar. O, why should wrath be mute, and fury dumb ?
I am no baby, I, that with base prayers

I should repent the evils I have done :
Ten thousand worse than ever yet I did
Would I perform, if I might have my will :
If one good deed in all my life I did,
I do repent it from my very soul.   190

Luc. Some loving friends convey the emperor hence,
And give him burial in his father's grave :
My father and Lavinia shall forthwith
Be closed in our household's monument.
As for that heinous tiger, Tamora,
No funeral rite, nor man in mourning weeds,
No mournful bell shall ring her burial ;
But throw her forth to beasts and birds of prey :
Her life was beastly and devoid of pity,
And, being so, shall have like want of pity.   200
See justice done on Aaron, that damn'd Moor,
By whom our heavy haps had their beginning :
Then, afterwards, to order well the state,
That like events may ne'er it ruinate.   *Exeunt*

Notes

I. i. 69. *Sound drums*, etc.; the stage directions are given for the most part as in Q, retaining the imperative.

I. i. 136-8. Hecuba and Polymnestor.

I. i. 177. " Call no man happy till he is dead."

I. i. 380. *wise Laertes' son*; Ulysses, in Sophocles' *Ajax*.

II. i. 17. *Prometheus . . .*; Prometheus stole fire from heaven to give to men, and was, as punishment, fettered by Zeus on a crag in the Caucasus.

II. i. 108. *Lucrece*; the wife of Collatine; she killed herself after being ravished by Tarquin.

II. i. 133, 5. Both quotations are from Seneca's *Hippolytus*.

II. iii. 22. See *Æneid* iv.

II. iii. 43. *Philomel*; see note in II. iv. 26.

II. iii. 63. Actæon, having seen Diana bathing, was changed by her into a stag and run down and killed by his own hounds.

II. iii. 231. *Pyramus*; finding at the trysting place a blood-stained kerchief he thought his lover Thisbe had been killed, and killed himself; she returned, and finding him dead, killed herself.

II. iv. 26. Tereus, king of Thrace, married to Progne, violated her sister, Philomela, and cut out her tongue. She worked her story on a sampler and sent it to her sister, who then killed her son Itylus and cooked him as a dish for her husband.

II. iv. 51. *Cerberus . . .*; Orpheus went down to Hades to recover his lost wife Eurydice, and charmed Cerberus, the watch-dog, to sleep by his music.

III. i. 17. '*urns*'; Hanmer's emendation of Qq, Ff 1. 2, 3, '*ruines*'; F 4, '*ruins*.'

III. i. 34-36. Q 2 reads '*or if they did marke, All bootlesse unto them*'; Ff, '*oh if they did heare They would not pitty me*'; Capell, '*or, if they did mark, All bootless unto them, they would not pitty me*,' etc.

III. i. 170. *castle*; perhaps *casque*.

III. i. 282-3. '*employ'd in this*,' etc.; Q reads *And Lavinia thou shalt be imployde in these Armes, Beare thou my hand sweet wench betweene thy teeth*: as does F with minor differences of spelling. It looks as though the original reading had been

> *And Lavinia thou shalt be imployde in this Armes*
> *Beare thou my hand sweet wench betweene thy [teeth]*

teeth having been deleted in favour of *Armes* which was then set in the wrong line.

III. i. 292. '*leaves*'; Rowe's emendation of Qq, Ff, '*loues*.' (perhaps better *lones*, i.e. *loans*).

III. ii. 27. "Infandum, regina, iubes renovare dolorem," *Æneid* ii.

IV. i. 82. *Magni Dominator . . .*; from Seneca's *Hippolytus*; "Lord of the great sky, can you hear of wickedness, and see it, so unmoved?"

IV. i. 106. *Sibyl's leaves*; the Sibyl's prophecies were written on leaves.

IV. ii. 20. *Integer vitæ . . .*; Horace, *Odes*, I. xxii., "He who is pure of life and clear of sin needs no Moorish bow and arrows."

IV. ii. 93. *Enceladus*; one of the Titans. *Alcides*; Heracles.

IV. ii. 98. *White-limb'd*: so both Q and F. Pope conjectured *white-lim'd*: which fits well enough with walls; but the whole phrase appears to have small applicability.

IV. iii. 4. '*Terras Astræa reliquit*'; Astræa was the goddess of Justice; (Ovid, *Metam.*, i. 150).

V. i. 42. An allusion to the old proverb, "A black man is a pear l in a fair woman's eye" (Malone).

V. iii. 73. ' *Lest Rome* '; Capell's reading; Qq, Ff, ' *Let Rome.*'

V. iii. 82. *Dido's sad attending ear* ; Æneas relates the story of the burning of Troy to Dido in the second book of the Æneid.

Glossary

MANY words and phrases in Shakespeare require glossing, not because they are in themselves unfamiliar, but for the opposite reason, that Shakespeare uses in their Elizabethan and unfamiliar sense a large number of words which seem so familiar that there is no incentive to look for them in the glossary. It is hoped that a glossary arranged as below will make it easy to see at a glance what words and phrases in any particular scene require elucidation. A number of phrases are glossed by what seems to be, in their context, the modern equivalent rather than by lexicographical glosses on the words which compose them.

Act First

SCENE I

line		line	
4	SUCCESSIVE TITLE, title to the succession	301	TRUST BY LEISURE, be slow to trust
16	DESERT IN PURE ELECTION SHINE, merit be rewarded by free election	304	STALE, dupe
		309	PIECE, 'piece of goods'
27	ACCITED, summoned	312	BANDY, quarrel
42	PRETEND, claim	313	RUFFLE, swagger
47	AFFY, trust	316	PHŒBE, the moon-goddess
61	CONFIDENT, trusting in	325	HYMENÆUS, god of marriage
121	PATIENT, make patient	333	PANTHEON, temple to all the gods
132	OPPOSE, compare		
178	HONOUR'S BED, i.e. the grave	351	RE-EDIFIED, rebuilt
182	PALLIAMENT, robe	352	SERVITORS, fighting-men
197	RIGHT, support	366	REPUTE, hold
226	TITAN, sun-god	368	NOT WITH, beside
238	ONSET, beginning	387	TROPHIES, emblems
259	FOR, on account of	430	INDIFFERENTLY, impartially
271	SITH, since	433	PUT IT UP, 'pocket it'

Act Second

SCENE I

line
- 3 OF, from
- 7 GALLOPS, gallops through
- 8 OVERLOOKS, looks over
- 14 MOUNT, mount to
  PITCH, height (to which a falcon rises before stooping)
- 22 SEMIRAMIS, a mythical queen of Assyria
- (25) BRAVING, quarrelling
- 41 LATH, property sword
- 62 BRABBLE, quarrel
- 64 JET, encroach upon
- 70 GROUND, *pun on* ground-bass

line
- 86 SHIVE, slice
- 88 WORN VULCAN'S BADGE, been cuckolded (as Vulcan was by Venus with Mars)
- 100 SQUARE, quarrel
- 104 FOR THAT, for all that
- 106 AFFECT, design
- 116 FITTED BY KIND, naturally fitted
- 117 SINGLE, separate (*hunting term*)
- 120 SACRED, accursed
- 123 FILE OUR ENGINES, polish our devices
- 126 FAME, rumour

SCENE II

- 3 BAY, baying

SCENE III

- 20 YELLOWING, yelling
- 32 DEADLY-STANDING, fixed in a stare like the eyes of the dead
- 53 BE CROSS, pick a quarrel
- 67 HORNING, cuckolding
- 69 ARE SINGLED FORTH, have separated yourselves from the company

- 211 UNCOUTH (unknown, *i.e.*) strange
- 222 EMBREWED, soaked in blood
- 236 COCYTUS, a river of hell
- 265 COMPLOT, plot
  TIMELESS, untimely

SCENE IV

- 5 SCROWL, gesticulate

Act Third

SCENE I

SCENE II

Act Fourth

SCENE I

SCENE II

SCENE III

line	line
33 WREAK, vengeance	various constellations and planets
44 ACHERON, one of the rivers of Hell	63 WELL SAID, well done
46 CYCLOPS, giants of Greek mythology	72 HORNS, the emblem of cuckoldry
52 THIS GEAR, these arms	92 TRIBUNAL PLEBS, *blunder for* tribunus (*or* tribunal) plebis
55-72 MERCURY, VIRGO, JUPITER, etc.,	113 LET ME ALONE, trust me

SCENE IV

3-4 FOR THE EXTENT OF EGAL JUSTICE, though extending impartial justice	21 ECSTASIES, madnesses
8 BUT EVEN, except what is consonant	42 GODDEN, good evening
	91 HONEY-STALKS, clover
	113 SUCCESSANTLY, in succession

Act Fifth

SCENE I

44 WALL-EY'D, ? with white of eye prominent	99 CODDING, eager to 'cod' (a *dial. word—*' to score off ')
88 LUXURIOUS, lustful	100 SET, trick

SCENE II

1 SAD, solemn	56 HYPERION, the sun-god
5 KEEPS, resides	87 WAGS, moves
11 SAD DECREES, solemn resolutions	

SCENE III